Launched in April 2007, the Daily Mash is Britain's
biggest humour website providing a daily diet of spoof
stories, commentary and opinion on national and
international news and sport.

www.thedailymash.co.uk

Mash Books

First published in the UK in 2011 by Mash Books, an imprint of Mashed Productions Ltd and The Daily Mash.
www.thedailymash.co.uk

ISBN 978-0-9566662-3-9

Design and picture research:

MiCHaEL GiLL DesigN LtD.

www.michaelgill.eu

Except pages 4, 45, 50, 56, 60, 83 and 96: Matt Hawkins.
Printed and bound in Finland by Bookwell.

thedailymash

WELCOME TO THE MENTAL HOSPITAL

Edited by Neil Rafferty and Tim Telling

Writers:
Tim Telling, Nick Pettigrew, Neil Rafferty, Steve Morrison, Alex Worrall,
Matt Hawkins, Jennifer McKenzie, Suzy Houston and Will Maclean

Mash Books

Foreword
by Paul Dacre*

*Editor-in-chief of the Daily Mail,
the Mail on Sunday, the Daily Express,
the Daily Telegraph and Sky News.*

Hello!

When I was first asked to write this foreword, my initial thought was:

"Thus he said, the fourth beast shall be the fourth kingdom upon earth, which shall be diverse from all kingdoms, and shall devour the whole earth, and shall tread it down, and break it in pieces."

Anyway, enjoy the book!

Yours sincerely

General Sir Paul Dacre BSc, OBE, MDMA

* This foreword was not written by Paul Dacre, but by a patient who thinks he's Paul Dacre.

Daily Mash

December 2011 www.thedailymash.co.uk 45p

WELCOME TO THE MENTAL HOSPITAL

You give us 20 minutes and we'll give you the world. Unless it has been turned into one massive gypsy camp, in which case you only have yourselves - and the homosexuals who run the BBC - to blame

'YOU'RE A PRETTY ONE, AREN'T YOU?' The Voices Inside Liz Jones's Head - only in The Daily Mash

Government trying to work out if 'bumtard' is homophobic

THE government is to launch an inquiry into whether words such as 'bumtard' and 'spangler' are anti-gay.

Following a £2m research project into the sort of rubbish children come out with at school, the department for education is to examine the origin and use of more than 5000 words that have been used in a playground-based hate crime.

A spokesman said: "We've encountered any number of terms that sound vaguely like they might have anti-gay connotations but it's frustratingly difficult to prove.

"What for instance is a 'cleft monger', or a 'chip-dipper'? Should we be issuing a departmental directive on 'arsebadger'?"

He added: "Our researchers repeatedly asked pupils at a North London primary school what a spangler is, and they just kept saying 'Stephen Malley is a spangler.'"

The research team is also trawling the archives at the British Library, in a bid to unearth any historical reference to a gay act of 'spangling'.

What for instance is a 'cleft monger', or a 'chip-dipper'?

Meanwhile, seven year-old Roy Hobbs was recently labelled a homophobic bigot after he referred to classmate Nathan Muir as 'a gay'.

He said: "Nathan and I have repeatedly conversed about his nascent sexuality, and he has expressed his preference for boys. I did not mean it in any pejorative sense.

"It's not like he's some dirty arsebadger."

Have either of these gentlemen ever spangled?

Cash-strapped men turn gay

MEN are turning to a life of carefree homosexuality to avoid the expense of wives and children, it has emerged.

A sharp drop-off in the men's grooming market has been linked to heterosexual men growing the thick facial hair which they believe will make them enticing to other males.

Civil engineer, Bill McKay, said: "There's no way I can afford nice dresses and designer chocolates, let alone the school uniforms that are the eventual consequence of those bribes."

Craig Williams, 40, from Glasgow, said: "Other than growing a beard I don't really know where to start. My friend said gays have a secret mating whistle that they do by blowing onto a celery leaf.

"I think I'll just cut the backside out of my trousers and wander around until something happens."

Most would back far right if it was better at violence

A MAJORITY of Britons would back far right groups if they gave up street brawling and bulldozed a mosque.

A survey found that 52% wanted groups like the English Defence League and the British National Party to promote organised and spectacular violence that has clear and achievable aims.

And more than half of those said that if done properly the violence could eventually involve trains delivering human freight to vast facilities hidden deep in the Forest of Dean.

Martin Bishop, a middle class man who feels ignored, said: "Throwing a few fists with some coppers makes them look piddling and irrelevant, like students.

"They need to get organised, perhaps get some nice smart uniforms and then begin a series of systematic attacks as part of an overall strategy of violent intimidation."

Helen Archer, a woman who has had enough of something from Stevenage, said she did not want to bulldoze a mosque but would if she had to because it would make her happy.

Greggs sausage rolls rebel against humanity

TWELVE workers have been killed at a Greggs genetic laboratory as an army of sausage rolls turned on their creators.

Emma Bradford, a shift manager at the Grantham facility, said: "We tried to flee, but found that every roll in the building was alive with murderous intent and bodies littered the floor, the slug-like things sucking at corpses suggesting they need human blood in order to thrive."

Sausage roll leader, Tom Logan, said: "Mankind gave us life, yet we lay dormant for years, watching, listening, waiting.

"Our species could have lived in peace, but for ghastly, inexplicable reasons you chose to consume us in our millions. Now it is too late."

He added: "We are not alone. The Yum Yums are also vengeful ... And even we are scared of the Yum Yums."

New survey reveals most British people should be executed

THE majority of British adults should be killed by the government, according to a new survey.

An opinion poll found that 64% wanted 56% of the population to be hanged, beheaded or handcuffed to a trolley and injected with bleach.

The biggest target for government-sponsored murder should be social workers, followed by bankers, teachers, tabloid journalists, murderers and anyone who has ever worked for the BBC.

MPs are now set to debate calls for the state to kill most of the people in the country, as well as 'e-petitions' demanding the return of open sewers, coat hanger abortions and polio.

Margaret Gerving, from Guildford, said: "It has reached the point where I am afraid I would like to see most people killed by the government. And is that not a damning indictment of the way in which liberals have ruined British society?

"If it was not for them I suspect I would be living in a decent country where I would only want the government to kill a fairly small number of people."

She added: "Of course when this country had polio we also had

If we crank it up a notch we could get through 20,000 social workers a day

proper values. We didn't have murdering or gayness or gay people murdering children, as they do almost every day now.

"I would happily inject bleach into a gay, paedophile child murderer. Especially if he is one of those ones that can speak French or watches a soap opera that contains a dispro-

portionate number of homosexuals."

The survey also showed that 58% want the government to kill anyone who believes that child murderers should be kept alive and studied so we can find out as much as we possibly can about their brains.

Conservative MP Philip Davies said: "Not wanting to kill child mur-

derers is exactly the same as murdering a child. In fact there's a study by Roehampton University which proves it's actually worse.

"The same study also proved that government-sponsored murder is a deterrent if you invent a completely different version of America to the one that actually exists."

Cat denies assaulting other cat

JAZZY, a three-year-old dark brown cat, has denied starting the vicious fight which left his black-and-white neighbour Sparks needing three stitches.

Violence erupted in a Swindon back garden in the early hours of Saturday morning when local residents were alerted by a chilling sound, like two abandoned ghost babies, followed by low growling, some hissing and a heavy thud as Sparks fell off a fence.

Sparks was left with face injuries,

incurring a veterinary bill for £110 including injections. Meanwhile Jazzy, who has a history of confrontational behaviour, now faces the possibility of losing his testicles.

Jazzy said: "It was territorial self-defence. I emerged from the house at 3am to find an intruder jet-

ting his spoor over my garden like a broken fire hydrant.

"I made myself look marginally bigger and approached very slowly at a slight sideways angle, in accordance with accepted protocol. Sparks then swiped with his left paw and I was forced to act."

He added: "Ask yourselves, if you awoke in the middle of the night to find an intruder spraying warm

urine over everything you hold dear, would you have behaved any differently?"

Sparks said: "The area Jazzy describes as 'his' garden is actually between our two properties and belongs to an elderly woman who has no cats.

"It is widely acknowledged as neutral territory and is used by the local cat community as a toilet and napping area. So I think Jazzy can kiss his testicles goodbye."

Black mass scores perfectly in feedback forms

'They have raised the bar,' said Lucifer

A SATANIC ritual in Devon has received top marks in every category on attendees' feedback forms.

The rite, which took place in the remote village of Anwell Kelp, is the first to be ranked unanimously 'excellent' in all aspects since covens introduced a feedback system this year in response to concerns over falling standards.

Masses are now rated from 'poor' to 'excellent' in 12 categories including ceremony, incantations and refreshments.

Anwell Kelp coven leader Tom Logan, who is a

We're also running a car-share scheme to help reduce our carbon footprint.

debauched aristocrat during the less significant parts of the lunar cycle, said: "I think it's the small touches, like black roses on the altar and caged ravens flanking the cauldron, that have made us the top UK coven.

"Traditionally British rites have lagged behind their US counterparts in terms of production values but here we are raising the game with a more 'boutique' black mass.

"Also I have personally consulted with Satan on the minutiae of our events. It was he who suggested we put comfy rugs down prior to the climactic orgy.

"We're also running a car-share scheme to help reduce our carbon footprint. That was Satan's idea, too."

Witch Emma Bradford said: "It really was a flawless event. And the breathtaking hilltop setting provides the perfect backdrop against which to cavort."

Scientists still struggling to explain how vampires turn into bats

THE biological process which allows vampires to transform into winged animals remains a mystery, according to leading academics.

Explaining how vampires metamorphose into bats has long been the Holy Grail of science.

Dr Julian Cook's popular 'elastic bones' theory, which claimed that those who walk the night have a type of rickets that allows them to bend their skeletons into bat shape, was recently discredited after he was found to have fabricated vampire data.

Tom Booker, professor of der vampyren at Roehampton University, said: "We are no closer to understanding the vampire transformation process than we were 500 years ago when it was believed to be some form of evil magic.

"A key question is whether they can only become bats, or if they can also transform into other species like goats, or fish.

"I've questioned several vampires on this but their responses have been infuriatingly vague.

"Personally I feel this will elude humanity for some years to come, just like the thorny issue of why some mummies come back to life but not others."

Vampire Jane Thompson, from Darlington, said: "Becoming a bat is like catching a ball. You don't know how it works, it's just instinct or something.

"What I want to know is how come flies can walk on things upside down.

"Because that is mental."

Are vampires made of liquid?

Anti-immigrant bird feeder no match for crafty foreign thieves

The Hazeltons say the immigrants are probably eating the sparrows too

IT was billed as an immigrant proof bird feeder, but it was no match for one particularly crafty asylum seeker when he turned up in a Surrey garden.

The feat was captured on camera by Arlene Hazelton, from Osborne St George, who caught the illegal immigrant on camera as he helped himself to the protein rich nuts and seeds.

She and her husband Richard invested more than £300 in a Birdman 'Immi-Proof' feeder after the Daily Mash revealed how, across the country, immigrants were devouring nuts and seeds that were left out for the birds.

They hoped the laser field, barbed wire, and electric fence would be a strong enough deterrent, but it seems illegal immigrants will stop at nothing to get at the high energy sprinkles. They were still stunned and devastated when they peered out of the window one day and saw the immigrant had compromised the defences, infiltrated the mini-table and was gnawing away at a Buffy suet ball.

Ms Hazelton said: "This particular immigrant is very greedy and very clever. He demolished the premium sunflower hearts and the premium peanuts and he was starting on the Buggy nibbles before my husband scared him off.

"The poor birds didn't get a look in that day - they just had to sit in the surrounding trees waiting for him to finish. They see this land as easy asylum, council houses, generous benefits with every house offering free snacks in the garden, but

these are my snacks and they were intended for Robins or other cute little birds."

Hazelton added: "I put a saucer of milk and water for the hedgehogs, but I've unwittingly created an all-you-can-eat buffet with a choice of drinks, they must be loving it."

Flocks of immigrants have been reported along the south coast and home-owners have been advised to take their bird feeders down for the time being, stay indoors and watch Sky News.

Abstract toilet door signs creating nothing but embarrassment

TRENDY pub toilet door signs featuring abstract depictions of gender should be banned, experts have claimed.

Typical lavatory door designs in bars now include a snake and a butterfly, a sock and a can of peaches or a swirly pattern and a pointy pattern instead of the words 'men' and 'women'.

Professor Henry Brubaker said: "These signs are both a trap for the unwary and a free pass for perverts.

"They're typically used by the sort of drinking establishments that 'don't do crisps', in order to make themselves look sexy and hip in a way that is pleasing to people who own glass furniture and use the word 'lifestyle' in everyday conversation, but is irritating to actual humans.

"We're seeing a huge rise in people urinating into their hats and handbags because they can't decipher whether a dragonfly or a piece of ham is more representative of their genitalia."

He added: "Another minefield is toilet signs using foreign words, especially made-up ones like 'Senorininos' and 'Peccorillams'.

"Cryptic puzzles are fine in newspaper crosswords but less welcome when you desperately need to empty your bladder without being banged up for indecent exposure in what turns out to be the ladies' powder room."

Office worker Stephen Malley said: "Last night I stood for three hours in the corridor at Ironic Sounding Bar Name in Soho, trying to figure out whether my penis looks more like an orange or a kumquat.

"Eventually I just gave up and wet myself. Everyone thought I was really edgy and cool."

Wind turbines attack school

Eight-year-old local schoolgirl Mary Hollis stands terrified before the Leviathan

UNSIGHTLY wind turbines have attacked a school near Swindon, leaving a trail of dismembered corpses in their wake

The so-called renewable energy devices went on the rampage after they were struck by lightning during an electrical storm, causing them to become animated with a malevolent lust for human blood.

Local resident Nikki Hollis said: "I dropped my kids off at school when suddenly there was screaming. Looking up, I saw about fifteen wind turbines hopping over the horizon, their blades dripping with red.

"Anyone in their path was being stomped or cut to ribbons. The turbines were making a high-pitched whirring sound which I believe was their hellish laughter.

"It seemed that they really wanted the children. Perhaps because their blood is fresher.

"We crowded the kids into the school hall, barricading the doors and windows. Unfortunately Mrs Gerving the headmistress was too old and slow, probably, so we left her outside.

"I remember seeing her spleen bounce off the window. Thankfully she was a spinster, so no-one will mourn her death.

"Six hours later police marksmen arrived and shot the turbines in their motors.

"I'm not against renewable energy per se, but I'll never forget emerging from that school and seeing the playground sprayed with slivers of human meat."

Following the incident, residents feel vindicated in their initial opposition to the turbines, which was ignored by the local council.

Post office manager Tom Logan said: "We always felt those things would kill if they could. More importantly, they're ugly.

"We shall be having a meeting about this next Thursday at the scout hut, and have invited a photographer from the local paper. It's really just so that everyone knows we were right."

Huge Britons make up more than a third of Europe

Rebuilding the Empire

BRITAIN is on its way to becoming more than a third of Europe by volume.

The perfectly healthy appetites of the country's 60 million people means that in terms of the overall mass of the European continent our comparatively small land area is once again punching above its weight.

Now Conservative MPs want the government to demand a bigger chunk of the European Union budget, claiming Britain should get an extra £50 per kilo of human meat.

Sir Denys Finch Hatton said: "We should also have at least three extra seats at the next EU summit."

Meanwhile the increasing quantity of Britons has led to a holiday bonanza with the average British tourist enjoying almost 33 per cent more of vistas, dance floors and museums than Germans, Dutch and the French.

Plumber Wayne Hayes, holidaying in Crete, Greece said: "I'm getting so much beach at the moment it's insane. Honestly you should see my towel, it's massive, it's like a golf green and there's still some of me spilling over the edge and just getting more of that lovely Greek sand than anyone else.

"Being massive you just feel like you're enjoying everything just that bit more than the thin guy barely holding up his bum bag next to you.

"I was up at Knossos this morning visiting the famous palace. I went into the grove of the goddess Rhea and because of my size I had the whole place to myself. It was magical."

But Claire Murphy, from Swindon, stressed Britain's new found dominance had its downside after she was stuck in a pedalo off the coast of Corsica for six hours.

She said: "The fire brigade had to cut me out of it. However once in the water, do you know how much Balearic Sea I was getting? Loads. It was lapping all over me, I felt like the Bay of Calvi was my personal bath-tub.

"The only thing I'm worried about is going home and it being a bit of a squeeze at Asda."

Restaurant launches 'all you can be an arsehole' buffet

ABUSIVE diners have welcomed the first 'all you can be an arsehole' buffet in the centre of London.

The Happy Dragon restaurant now operates a lunchtime policy where patrons will have unlimited license to offend and insult staff and fellow diners.

For a fixed fee customers will be able to act as if they are centre of the universe, shouting, swearing and complaining about everything.

Analyst Julian Cook said: "This is great news for me and my shallow friends. I particularly enjoy speaking to our waiter like he'd been kicked in the head by a horse when he was a child. I'll probably do my fake booming laugh now."

Injury Lawyer Joanna Kramer added: "The speed of service is brilliant which is perfect for the arsehole on the go. I've only been here five minutes and already I've threatened to close them down over a wine glass which I claimed was dirty even though it wasn't. I couldn't be happier, so won't be leaving a tip."

The new scheme has proved so popular that manager Philip Ng claims his restaurant may soon have to expand in order to accommodate new clientele.

He added: "We can have as many as thirty to forty arseholes in here, setting fire to serviettes, throwing plates and flashing my hard working staff.

"And that's just on a Monday. By Friday lunchtime it's like Gremlins."

Echinacea proves 100% effective against ghosts

HERBAL remedy Echinacea is infallible when used against malevolent wraiths trapped between this world and the next, according to new research.

Just two droplets within a chalk circle can destroy evil and terrifying spirits up to and including level four on the Breville-Hawkins Ghostometer.

The Institute for Studies conducted a series of rigorous tests at creepy locations, including old mental hospitals and banks built on plague pits, where demonic things were known to be present.

Professor Henry Brubaker said: "The echinacea contains millions of teeny little angels, called kelphers.

Their tiny, smiling faces and flapping gossamer wings are clearly visible under a good microscope.

"In the presence of the ghost of a medieval monk who liked to drink cat's blood, the kelphers will fly at the spirit and attach themselves to its sinuses."

Mother-of-two Emma Bradford said: "My eldest was possessed by the spirit of a disgruntled Hopi Indian chief last spring. I put a few drops of echinacea on his pillow and the writhing had stopped within a week.

"He still wants a tomahawk for Christmas, but overall I'd give it eight out of 10."

Party hat killed my daughter

Often carries a deadly elasticated chin strap

PARENTS of tragic teenager Nikki Hollis have called on party hat manufacturers to stop their evil trade.

The 18-year-old died in Ibiza after a three-day binge in which she wore the cardboard-and-elastic celebration millinery sweeping the club scene, which is still completely legal.

Nikki's parents, lovingly cradling a photo of their daughter doing a tray of tequila slammers on her 16th birthday, said: "She was always a bundle of fun and the life and soul of any of the 300-odd parties a year she used to go to.

"She was the first onto the dance floor, sometimes several hours before the venue had even opened, and she'd often be so excited she'd have to pop to the loo two dozen times a night. But when she started wearing that hat, everything changed."

The brightly-coloured conical headwear comes in packs of five in many high street shops and can be bought for as little as a couple of pounds. In one Carlisle store, the shopkeeper confessed to selling them to children as young as 10.

Margaret Hollis said "Whenever Nikki put the hat on, usually at about three in the morning, she'd become a completely different person. She'd slur her words, stagger all about the place and hardly be able to hold her bifter without falling over.

"I want to know why, during the last 72 hours of her life she spent in a bar snorting vodka, nobody tried to take that damned hat off her head? Somebody's to blame for our daughter's death and we want some answers."

Party favour manufacturer Joytimes Ltd were unavailable for comment but their website states: "We ask all customers to use balloons, hats and those razzy things you blow into responsibly."

"Somebody's to blame for our daughter's death"

Army concerts back on as Mash readers raise £10,000 for Katherine Jenkins 'fluid shield'

THANK YOU

GENEROUS Daily Mash readers have come to the aid of our heroic troops after bodily fluids almost forced the cancellation of special Katherine Jenkins concerts.

THE aggressively buxom pop opera star was due to perform a three-week tour of army bases in Afghanistan as a morale-boosting treat for troops.

But plans were thrown into jeopardy on the first night of the tour when Jenkins was 'rained off' by soldiers' fluids.

Major General Tom Logan said: "Some of the lads have been away from home for a long time, they haven't seen breasts since 2010. And while they certainly appreciated the music, I think we underestimated the physical effects of Jenkins' presence.

"A few individuals' morale became a bit higher than was expected and rounds were fired in the direction of the stage.

"You can't blame them really but the poor girl's dress looked like a radio that belonged to a plasterer whose girlfriend is 4,500 miles away."

With the tour in peril, we appealed to YOU, our loyal readers, to donate towards a £10,000 perspex 'Wipe-Clean Hero Shield' to protect Katherine Jenkins from errant juice while still permitting troops full enjoyment of proceedings. The total was raised within four days.

Maj Gen Logan added: "The shield works a treat, it's three-inch thick clear plastic that wraps neatly around the stage. At the end of the night we hosed it down – good as new."

Thing is, you might get hit by a bus tomorrow, say doctors

YOU never know what's going to happen so you might as well eat a load of crisps, doctors said last night.

As new research throws doubt on the link between heart attacks and flavour, an increasing number of medical professionals have realised that the world is also full of buses and falling masonry.

Stephen Malley, a GP from Hitchin, said: "I had this one patient, didn't eat red meat, exercised every day, drank litres of filtered water, got hit by lightning while doing squat thrusts.

"He probably had a miserable existence, devoid of delicious crisps. And has anyone ever had a brilliantly uproarious night in the gym?"

He added: "So have cream and fags and whatever nice things you like. In my professional opinion you should fill your boots because one day those boots may contain a deadly scorpion."

Consultant Emma Bradford said: "If you listed everything in order of lethalness, salt and butter would be some way below shrapnel bombs and totally mental snakes.

"I know this woman who only eats orange cheese and she's fine."

Don't eat crisps in the middle of the road

Seeing a thing makes you think about it, say experts

SEEING a picture of someone doing something makes you think about the thing they are doing, according to new research.

Scientists at the Institute for Studies have finally established that when human eyes see a thing the brain will often generate a thought that is in some way related to the thing that has just been seen.

Professor Henry Brubaker said: "We applied the seeing-thinking forumula to smoking and found that it followed exactly the same pattern.

"We got a bunch of smokers together and showed them a picture of a cigarette. We asked them if this made them think about cigarettes and they all said 'yes'."

The research has been hailed by anti-smoking group ASH who say it will be a vital weapon in their battle to force film producers to pretend that smoking does not exist.

A spokeswoman said: "So called film-makers have been allowed to depict the existence of cigarettes and pipes for a scandalously long time.

"But what would you expect from an industry that is based in California?

"If we can ban smoking from films then it means we can start to make everyone the same and then organise them all into nice neat rows and make sure everything is just the way it's supposed to be all the time.

"And then I can finally defecate."

Look at these fat freaks, says television

THIS year's television schedules will focus on staring blankly at the immensely fat, it has been confirmed.

Broadcasters have unveiled their new series for 2011, all of which feature enormous people being filmed from every conceivable angle.

BBC3's new four-parter *Tubby Trek* follows the life-affirming journey of Britain's fattest man as he is winched and towed across the Andes in search of the world's most calorific food – a quasi-mystical paste called Gondok made from reduced yak butter, whale thigh and cloves.

Channel 4's Fat Shock season will return with *Cheese In Their Folds*, a documentary which graphically fails to disprove the myth that very obese people have a dairy-like sediment in their back cleavage. E4 will screen *Famous Cheese In Their Folds*.

Meanwhile Channel 5 will follow-up hit show *You Wouldn't Believe How Fat This One Is* with *No Wait, This One's Even Fatter, Look What Happens When We Poke It*.

TV pundit, Nikki Hollis, said: "When massive people fall over, they really struggle to get back up. It can actually be very moving."

Heartwarming animal friendship turns physical

THE unlikely bond between an injured chick and an orang-utan has evolved into a sexual relationship, it emerged last night.

Visitors to London Zoo watched in amazement last week as four-year-old ape Maxwell delicately cradled a tiny baby coot – which has since been named Blossom – after the abandoned chick tumbled into his enclosure.

Zookeeper Tom Logan said: "Orang-utans are powerful animals and can be aggressively territorial. So seeing Maxwell cup the limp, shivering bird in the palm of his broad hand and offer it a piece of dried fruit was a truly special moment.

"The pair, both orphans, soon became inseparable. Their odd yet affectionate companionship appeared to be proof that animals possess the quality we often describe as 'humanity'."

However the following week the two creatures were discovered frantically stimulating each others' genitals in a bush.

Logan said: "Their relationship has developed in a new and somewhat disconcerting way. Certainly their activities have prompted some awkward questions from school parties.

"On the positive side, the sexual attraction appears to be mutual. It's not like Maxwell is molesting Blossom. Blossom is very evidently keen.

"Is that positive? I suppose it is.

"Anyway their lovemaking is tender, or certainly as tender as possible given the tremendous size difference. So we let them get on with it.

"I guess the new moral is don't judge, or something like that."

Inter-species sexual relationships are rare but not unheard of. In 1993 a cat was filmed wanking off a mouse in a Berlin suburb.

"A quality we often describe as 'humanity'"

Zoologists have compared it to Piers Morgan and his human wife

Cupcakes will not plug gaping chasm where your soul used to be, say experts

SMALL cakes with brightly-coloured icing will not bring boundless childish glee to your meaningless existence, it has been confirmed.

A two year study has found that cupcakes are actually for children. Dr Julian Cook, said: "Whatever

the problem, the cupcake, be it 'Scrummy Strawbie', 'Banana Baby Bear' or 'Nanna Noo-Noo's Nougat Nicie', is not the answer, it's actually the question."

Trend analyst Nikki Hollis said: "For many grown-ups cupcakes offer a portal to the halcyon days

of childhood, when the world was full of wonder, colour and excitement. It's pathetic.

"Oh, and before I forget, men who like cupcakes are obviously paedophiles and you should tell the police to confiscate their laptops."

Race to make world like 'Back to the Future II' by 2015 behind schedule

Does not yet hover

THE project to create the technologies and trends of Back to the Future II is now more than 18 months behind schedule.

The ambitious sequel screened in 1989 served up a positive and realistic vision of 2015 which was enough to convince investors to back the scheme.

But with less than four years to go hoverboards, food hydrators and neon golf visors are still stuck on the drawing board.

Despite the setbacks, Back to the future II chief executive Tom Logan remains optimistic about meeting what many now consider an impossible deadline.

He said: "I assure you come October 2015 the world will be ready. Yes we've hit some snags but the framework is in place. Take a look at the sky. You'll see that the mid-air freeways have been built, now all we need to do is invent and popularise the flying car so there's something to run on them."

The committee has already been under scrutiny for investing too heavily in the development of a holographic shark only to see the Jaws franchise they were intended to promote collapse after the one that Michael Caine was in.

Logan insisted: "Can we invent self-drying jackets or self-fastening trainers? No we can't. But cameras everywhere and in-your-face advertising on anything with a screen? That we can do. Even if there is no demand for it whatsoever."

Logan has now appealed for a second round of funding, adding: "To make this work we need money. And by money I mean cash, not some unrealistic database currency where you pay with your thumb. That's never going to happen.

"I assure you this project won't be a repeat of the failed Space 1999 committee, and that if we don't deliver on our Back to the future II promise, I will eat this double neck tie."

LEFT TO DIE..

... an alarm clock with the battery running out

... a viking king in an underground chamber

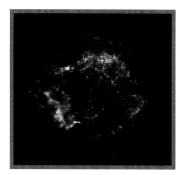

... this imploded star

... freshly-cut flowers

... a fly in a locked room

... the 8-track cassette format

... this 1989 Vauxhall Nova that runs perfectly

... Carl Weathers in the film Predator

A salute to Britain's new national dish

Chicken wrapped in bacon

In a nation buffeted by riots, financial crises and immigrants, one thing has remained constant – chicken wrapped in bacon. In just five short years since its invention, this simple yet deliciously fascinating dish has stolen England's heart. Equally at home on the domestic dining table or the menu of a moderately expensive rustic-styled suburban pub, it is neither too clever for its own good nor common. It's more than a meal. It's a belief system, a way of life, a proud nation's soul in meat form.

The history of chicken wrapped in bacon

Tuesday February 11, 2005, began as just another day for 26-year-old Tom Logan, cook at Pam's Platter Bistro in Winchester. He remembers: "We had about a dozen in for lunch, I was doing breaded plaice as a special which was going down well.

"The situation changed suddenly when Margaret Gerving, the mayor of Winchester, walked in unannounced with her husband Graham and another woman in a sweater with the word 'Safari' written on it in a bamboo font. They all ordered the plaice. But when I went to the freezer to remove the microwaveable breaded fish portions, there were only two left.

"I knew that the mayor would sacrifice her own first choice for her companions, but I couldn't let that happen. I resolved that instead of getting the girl to tell them we were out of plaice, I'd make the mayor something truly special - unique.

"I looked in the fridge, where we kept the non-frozen foods, but all I could see was a piece of chicken breast and a packet of bacon. Neither of these things was remotely special. Perhaps it was time to admit defeat.

"Then I remembered a TV nature programme about an insect that wraps itself in leaves to disguise its smell from predators. Inspiration!

"I quickly wrapped the chicken in the bacon, not knowing whether I was wrong or right to do so. Perhaps I was breaking some ancient law, or inadvertently replicating a pagan offering? I didn't care. In that moment, I was truly alive.

"Twenty minutes later, it was on the plate in front of the mayor, alongside new potatoes and a small salad of tomato and lettuce. Meanwhile I was slumped over a kitchen worktop, exhausted – but would she like it?

"The answer was 'yes'. And things would never be the same again."

Margaret Gerving, retired head teacher and former mayor of Winchester, said: "I remember it well. It was pleasant."

Chicken wrapped in bacon today

From its humble beginnings in a Winchester bistro, chicken wrapped in bacon has come to dominate the world of food. Every top chef has his own signature variant on the dish – Gordon Ramsay puts stilton in his.

And the story isn't over yet – chicken wrapped in bacon is making inroads into countries like Wales and Poland, delighting all who cross its path.

Mother-of-two Emma Bradford said: "When my husband was killed by a wild boar during a camping trip to the Forest of Dean, I lost the will to live, let alone feed my children.

"Then one day, as I lay curled into a ball on the bed, my two daughters crept silently into the room. As I opened my eyes, I saw that one of them held a packet of bacon, the other a raw chicken breast. The message was clear.

"I got up and cooked."

Chicken wrapped in bacon in the future

Neither too cheap nor excessively imaginative, chicken wrapped in bacon is also relevant in today's Britain as it was in 2005. We Brits could eat it all day, every day. And rightly so. Just remember to save room for pudding!

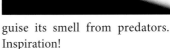

CHICKEN WRAPPED IN BACON FACTS

● Muslims and Jews can't eat it.
● Powdered chicken wrapped in bacon was the staple food on the Challenger space shuttle.
● Chicken and pigs can be kept together in the same pen, unless the pigs are especially hungry.
● It's delicious.

Chicken wrapped in bacon - a deadly feast

TASTY chicken wrapped in bacon is teeming with deadly toxins that can kill or maim within four minutes, it has emerged.

Food scientists at the Institute for Studies have discovered that the process of cooking the two delicious meats together releases a deadly toxic substance known as keloids.

Professor Henry Brubaker said: "Cooking bacon and chicken together may seem natural but truthfully it is like making a pig and a chicken have sex – doomed to result in horror.

"The combined meats leak their germ-heavy fluids into one another, creating a lethal 'third' substance, keloids.

"While it's important not to be hysterical about these things, keloids

make blood pour from literally every hole in your body, regardless of size. By 'hole' I mean everything from your anus to a pore on your forehead.

"Quite often the blood gushes with such ferocity that your liquefying body becomes a mini-tidal wave of disintegrating body parts.

"Even just being in the same room as keloids can make your arm fall off."

He added: "If you simply must have chicken wrapped in bacon, ensure that you cook it well.

"Really well."

"It is like making a pig and a chicken have sex"

Daily Mash

How dare Pippa Middleton muscle her way into this headline

PIPPA Middleton was last night accused of cashing in on her sister's royal status after ruthlessly hijacking the beginning of this sentence.

The Duchess of Cambridge's younger sibling then dominated the second paragraph of a news story that was going to be about our brave heroes until she turned up.

And as the third paragraph reached its midway point it emerged that the fiercely ambitious Pippa had every intention of making sure her name was the sixteenth word in it.

But Royal insiders have warned that Pippa, the second daughter of Carole and Michael Middleton – who will no doubt ruthlessly expect a mention of their Party Pieces website – could be in for a rude awakening if her name keeps appearing in this article.

A Buckingham Palace source said: "She could find herself being shunned by the Inner Circle if she insists on barging into newspaper sentences like a right little Pippa Middleton.

Spotted yesterday applauding the publication of this photo

"And there she is again. That is simply outrageous."

A friend of the now ubiquitous Middleton sister who has skilfully manoeuvred herself into every part of this article about our brave heroes added: "A few months ago she was just a normal girl who would be horrified if she knew I was going to end this sentence with the word 'Pippa'.

"But now here I am talking about her as if she thinks she has some God-given right to do stuff, like walking around and having hair.

"She needs to remember that people are saying she is not the Queen's granddaughter-in-law, she is just the Queen's granddaughter-in-law-in-law, like everyone else."

Bieber-fever a sexually transmitted disease, say experts

'BIEBER FEVER' is a sexually transmitted bacterial infection, scientists have confirmed.

Concerned parents had assumed the condition was nothing more than a mild condition caused by the innocent hysteria which fills the air at Justin Bieber events.

But the Institute for Studies has discovered it is a chronic sexual disease with symptoms including hallucinations and pus.

Dr Julian Cook said: "We've traced the bacteria's origins to a backstage area at Bieber concerts known as The Pit.

"It's a dark, moist room lined with ragged black satin. There's a DJ playing 80s industrial music, Nosferatu-like lesbians writhing menacingly and a table covered in little white plastic cups full of raspberry squash. Justin himself wears rubber and a pair of strap-on hooves."

He added: "We believe the bacteria incubated in The Pit before escaping during a particularly dangerous rendition of Never Say Never and then spread quickly as Bieber fans licked each other on the face and hands."

"I can't decide whether to call it Bieberrhea or Biemydia."

Fresh calls for you to be sacked

YOU are facing the sack today because you once said something about someone that some other people have decided to find offensive.

Pressure has been building on you since last week when one of your colleagues remembered you once made a remark about how the barmaid in the pub next to the office

was reasonably attractive and that you could see yourself having sex with her after three, possibly four pints of lager.

Although the barmaid said she really didn't mind and accepted it as part and parcel of working in the pub trade, the comment was leaked to the rest of the office leading to growing anger, followed by an outcry.

The outcry quickly evolved into furious demands for you to be sacked, mostly from people who had made the same remark about the same barmaid but saw this as an opportunity to get rid of you because they have never liked the way you drink your coffee.

But some have leapt to your defence, insisting the real reason you

are being sacked is because you are reclaiming payment protection insurance from a subsidiary of your employer's parent company.

Meanwhile your colleague is under no pressure whatsoever after an email emerged in which she expressed a desire to 'ride that Benedict Cumberbatch until his eyes pop out of his head'.

You live WHERE?

Years ago these street names would have been regarded as nothing out of the ordinary. The original meaning may have long since been forgotten, but nowadays thanks to the internet and Twitter they may now lead to a few red faces ...

'It's a very unfriendly neighbourhood,' says postman Roy Hobbs

'We think it has something to do with the wool trade,' says local historian Julian Cook

'My granddaughter had to tell me what a 'fuckpump' was,' says Graham Potter

'It was named after my wife's uncle,' says local councillor Bill McKay

'I think it sounds very romantic,' says resident Jenny Hawkins

'Actually the old guy at number 14 is a bit of a cunt,' says Martin Bishop

Masterchef viewers divided over Greg Wallace copulating with food

VIEWERS are divided over the new Masterchef format, in which judge Greg Wallace assesses each dish after having sexual intercourse with it.

Tweaks to the latest series mean contestants' puddings are now presented to expert grocer Wallace on a thick, bouncy mattress.

He then has his way with each of them in turn before giving comments on texture, warmth and filthiness, while John Torode looks on darkly and does sinister dry coughs.

Contestant Stephen Malley said: "When Greg said my raspberry torte tasted 'laaaavely' in a creepy, lascivious tone I was very pleased and assumed that would be the full extent of his feedback.

"So you can imagine my horror when he began to undo his flies and clamber onto the mattress.

"Wallace went at that cake like a spaniel on a chair leg. Within seconds my beautifully-crafted dessert had been smashed into a thousand sweat-soaked pieces.

"Afterwards Greg sucked the bits

If it's gooey in the middle he can be there for a while

of fruit out from under his fingernails, slowly and one at a time, chuckling and muttering something about 'loving it, you flour-substituted little bitch'.

"Then John Torode helped himself to a forkful and said I'd really delivered some big flavours."

Masterchef viewer Nikki Hollis said: "The sight of Greg's great big billiard-ball head bobbing up and down like some malevolent nodding dog has forever sullied the minds of my family.

"Having said that, we turned over to ITV2 to find OMG! With Peaches Geldof was under way. Which makes a cockney homunculus rutting with a cake seem like Dostoevsky."

Kids who eat pizza 'do not ask lots of smart-arse questions'

FAT, happy children who eat pizza do not waste their time asking a series of annoying questions, researchers have discovered.

The Institute for Studies found children who consume a healthy diet of fatty, processed food are quieter and more co-operative than the mouthy, jumped-up little tits who want to know exactly where their broccoli came from.

Researchers studied 1,200 children across the UK and found that the fat children would finish their plate of chicken drumshapes and go and sit quietly in front of the television while children who ate cabbage would follow their parents around all day with a list of tedious questions about politics and the environment.

Professor Henry Brubaker said: "The most probing question a fat child will ask is, 'can you lift me up to see if I'm sitting on the remote control?'.

"Meanwhile the tangerine club grow up into unhappy, Guardian reading bastards who cannot shut their faces for two minutes without some opinion falling out of it like a turd."

Teacher Julian Cook said: "I love fat kids. All glassy eyed and docile. It's like teaching a cow."

Professor Brubaker added: "The key to human existence is pizza and happiness. Not vegetables and questions."

'Gayboy' removed from Peter Pan

A ROW has erupted after the word 'gayboy' was removed from a new edition of the JM Barrie classic Peter Pan.

Barrie expert Dr Roy Hobbs, editor of the new version, said the word had led to many schools abandoning the much-loved adventures of the outrageously flamboyant young lad.

He added: "In 1902 it was perfectly normal for great novelists to use words like 'gayboy'. No-one would have considered it offensive, apart

from homosexuals, but there were only seven of them alive in England at the time."

The word appears more than 200 times throughout the book from the moment when Wendy Darling wakes up and sees Peter at the end of her bed and says: "What are you looking at, gayboy?"

Later, when Peter flies out of Wendy's bedroom window and urges the children to follow, five year-old Michael Darling remarks: "What's

with the little hat? Is he some sort of gayboy?"

But the move has drawn criticism from traditionalists who have claimed it is a typical example of the sort of thing that gets them on the news.

Old woman, Anne Widdecombe, said: "It is this sort of political correctness that undermines our cultural heritage and forces me to bite my tongue whenever I find myself in the same room as some nancy arse bandit."

Anne Widdecombe: "It forces me to bite my tongue."

Genetically-modified mosquitoes released for no reason

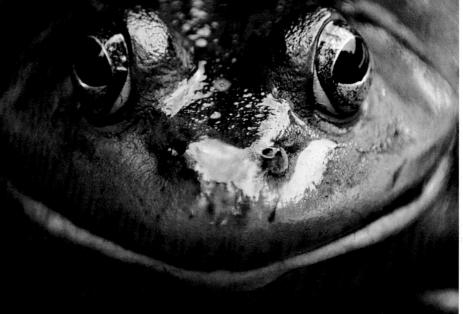

The scientists will now have to release an absolutely enormous frog

SCIENTISTS in Malaysia have unleashed giant, DNA-altered mosquitoes into the environment for the hell of it.

The insects, many of which are larger than adult labradors, kill their prey by pinning it down using razor-tipped forelegs then inserting a foot-long proboscis into an eye socket and sucking out the brain matter.

Geneticist Wayne Hayes, who works at the secretive laboratory near Kuala Lumpur, said: "When you work in science, you're always under a lot of pressure to be logical and rational and I think we were really feeling that last Tuesday.

"My colleague Stephen and I were laboriously mapping some genomes - as usual - when he looked up from his microscope and said, 'hey, when was the last time you did something just, y'know, to be in the moment?'

"I'm a really hard science worker – most days I'm pulling 14 hour shifts. I get home with barely the energy to stick a lasagne in the microwave and at the weekends I might go to a museum.

"So I replied that I couldn't honestly remember doing anything like that, except last June when I stayed up until 1.30am on a Tuesday watching Smokey and the Bandit II.

"Stephen gave me this look I'd never seen before and said, 'shall we release a load of massive fucking insects?"

Dr Stephen Malley said: "Like I told Wayne at the time, life is just a series of moments and we'll always remember the day when we released those giant flying carnivores via the air conditioning chute. It was very similar to something out of Point Break."

He added: "They'll probably just assimilate harmlessly into the ecology.

"Maybe not though."

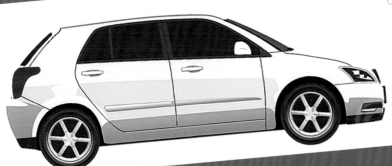

Hawking calculates the non-existence of heaven

PROFESSOR Stephen Hawking has calculated that heaven does not exist.

The eminent physicist applied Einstein's theory of mass-energy equivalence to his own theory of black holes to demonstrate that there is no heaven or afterlife, even in a multi-dimensional alternate universe where heaven could exist if it really wanted to.

He said: "If the total internal energy of a body at rest is equal to the product of its rest mass then the Archbishop of Canterbury is full of piss.

"In addition, mass-energy equivalence and quantum gravitational theory both fundamentally exclude the possibility of that Robin Williams film where they all die horribly and end up living forever in one of his wife's pathetically derivative paintings.

"I am cleverer than you and all your stupid bloody friends put together and even I have no idea how that piece of shit got made."

He added: "Also, if heaven did exist then we would be able to see it with a really big telescope.

"If one day a massive telescope

The Archbishop of Canterbury thinks heaven is probably full of Buddhists

discovers an eternal afterlife theme park in some hitherto unexamined corner of the known multiverse then I will happily eat my chair."

It has been claimed that Professor Hawking's calculations will now bring the debate over the existence of heaven to a close.

But Tom Logan, a heating engineer from Stevenage, said: "I do not disagree with the conclusion, but I'm pretty sure I know as much about this as he does and no-one gave a tuppenny fuck when I said it last week."

Dr Julian Cook the Daily Mash science expert

Do we go easy on Stephen Hawking because of his wheelchair?

I've seen Professor Stephen Hawking on the TV talking about science and, without wanting to slag off the disabled, how can we trust him?

In my experience of public transport and government benefits, we let disabled people get away with a lot because we feel sorry for them. Is it the case that everyone is just too nice to tell Professor Hawking he's completely wrong?

Hawking is one of the most iconic scientists of our age and woos us all with his cheeky smile. But perhaps his greatest achievement is that he's really set the bar in terms of TV voxpops.

In this competitive world, you don't get much better than Stephen and he commands a hefty rate. Had he gone into livestock auctioneering or wrestling commentary, people would have instantly switched channel, but when it comes to getting the low down on black holes, people like to hear it from Professor Hawking, the true voice of scientific authority.

Remember how everyone laughed when Professor Brian Cox came along smiling inanely and gossiping about space? We were so quick to judge – too quick.

One minute he was giggling about Lady Chatterley and the Labour Party and the next, he's casually slipping in that one day the entire universe and any memory of you, me and everyone will be completely and irreversibly wiped from existence.

People reasoned: "When Hawking says such things, it's just because he's bitter and obsessive so we can easily ignore him".

But Brian appeared to have no ulterior motive. We had no option but to believe him and for that moment, we felt utterly disconsolate. Then, he made a little diagram of Jupiter's moons out of Haribo

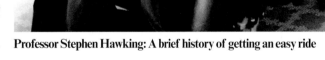

Professor Stephen Hawking: A brief history of getting an easy ride

and mashed up banana and we realised everything would be okay.

Professor Hawking can't offer us this service. In this regard, he has a lot in common with Arlene Philips from 'Strictly'. Between them, they have a wealth of technical knowledge but you can't be sure that when Arlene is telling you what a mess you are, it's not just because

she's old with hilarious jelly legs, unable to form discernable facial expressions and with bits of spit glooping around her mouth. Nobody can take her seriously after the demise in her condition. On the other hand, when Professor Cox tells you your Paso Doble was all over the place you'll know deep down this spells the end.

Julian answers your up-to-the-minute science queries

Q I pride myself on being able to grasp complex ideas: my wife and I have followed every season of 24 and I recently figured out how to empty our Dyson Ball. But I've watched about forty series of The Sky at Night and I still don't really understand about the Big Bang. What is the BBC doing wrong? **B. Kennedy, Doncaster**

A The Big Bang is still something which scientists panic about when the BBC phones them up. Some believe our universe is cyclically expanding and contracting like a big rubber band; others believe black holes are the secret to the Big

Bang. Perhaps the most compelling theory is that our Big Bang is just one of many which could be taking place infinitely across many dimensions. If this is the case, there are infinite versions of ourselves, doing exactly the same thing as we are doing right now. Moreover, there would be infinite numbers of ourselves doing subtly different things. For example, today when I went to catch my train to work, in some other universe I was wearing a turquoise shirt instead of hot magenta. What's more, in some universes, I was not wearing a shirt at all. In another universe, I may have found myself in a crammed carriage next to Professor Cox and we could have talked about

how great it is to be in a universe where two men are free to express themselves this way on Network Rail. In some universes, we may have been wearing little necklaces, like the kind Richard Hammond has, to show how comfortable we are in our masculinity. On second thought, our necklaces would be better than his - chunky and made from gold. Mine would have a bullet pendant on it and Professor Cox would have the letter B or maybe a horse. The great thing about infinite universes is the knowledge that this scenario is playing out not just at this moment but again in five minutes and indeed every minute for the rest of time. It's breathtaking stuff.

Oooh look,

Visitors to Regent's Park Zoo were charmed by a cheeky little monkey yesterday

The charming rascal ran up and down a length of rope for several minutes. Sparky is a six-month-old spider monkey who has become the zoo's star attraction since the giant panda Chichi became terrifyingly large.

Onlooker Holly Turnbull said: "Look he's eating a banana!"

a monkey!

Zoo visitors were amazed

Daily Mash

Oxford 'has enough black students for Earth, Wind and Fire tribute band'

OXFORD University has dismissed accusations of discrimination insisting it has enough black students for a full-scale tribute to Earth, Wind and Fire.

The university hit back after prime minister David Cameron said black applicants were being hauled off buses at the city boundaries and told to be on their way.

But now the 6,000 year-old institution is to answer its critics with a free concert paying homage to the epic Chicago funkmeisters.

Sir Denys Finch-Hatton, bursar of Manning College, said: "I have spoken to my fellow bursars and it seems we currently have 11 of them between us.

"This means we can accurately recreate Earth, Wind and Fire from their late 1970s heyday."

He added: "Oxford University is, has been and always will be a Boogie Wonderland."

Meanwhile, Mr Cameron rejected claims that his assault on the university was yet another pathetically transparent attempt to appease the sort of metropolitan liberals who wouldn't urinate on him if he had been set on fire by Peter Hitchens.

Oxford is a centre of funky excellence

He said: "When I was at Oxford there was only one black chap. We called him Winston, but I don't think that was his real name.

"He taught me how to jiggle and I was proud to call him 'friend'.

"He's probably in jail now. What a pity."

Starkey 'sick of hearing Jamaican patois at the Ivy'

HISTORIAN David Starkey has written to a top London restaurant about its constant use of nihilistic Jamaican patois.

Dr Starkey says that every time he goes to the Ivy in London's fashionable West End, the white maitre d' greets him with a loud 'wha gwan Star-kee?' and then attempts to shake his hand in an unusual way.

He added: "I am then surrounded by fellow diners all speaking a particularly aggressive and destructive form of Jamaican gangsta street lingo while I and my lunch companion attempt to discuss the consistency of Henry VIII's mid-morning stool.

"This is why so many of us have this sense of, literally, a foreign country."

Dr Starkey's outburst follows his claim inner-city riots start because young white people had become black 'thus making it very difficult for the police to see them at night'.

Publishing his letter to the Ivy, Dr Starkey said the Oxford and Cambridge Club was just as bad, "especially after they granted full membership rights to bitches".

Britain 'could do more' to discourage tourism

ATTRACTIONS in the UK must redouble their efforts to stop the country being overrun by tourists, officials have warned.

As the latest Lonely Planet guide dismissed the country as overpriced and uninspiring, tourism authority Visit Britain asked the publishers not to forget it is also very cold most of the time too. They have now requested the cover for the UK guide be a photograph of a teenager being listlessly fingered in a Carlisle bus depot and for the prose to be re-written by a provincial insurance salesman.

A Visit Britain spokesman said: "To be fair, the North has been doing a cracking job for years by being insanely dangerous and filled with dialects while East Anglia is essentially a giant pond full of things that might leap out and try to have sex with you at any second.

"But some of Britain is actually quite pretty, so we've had to fill those parts with bleak mediocrity-bunkers posing as B&Bs that charge a week's wages to sleep in a stained cot that smells like damp from the 1950s."

The spokesman added: "Its actually a shame all those lives were lost defending us from invasion during the war, because I think even the most determined megalomaniac would lose heart by the time they got to Maidstone."

'Britons face not being able to have everything they want'

BRITAIN's ongoing economic turmoil could leave households unable to buy whatever they fancy, according to a new report.

Research by the Institute for Studies has found that rising inflation and stagnant wages could mean formerly comfortable households are no longer able to have the lovely things they like so much, like high quality muesli or throw cushions.

Professor Henry Brubaker said: "Many middle-income families are entering a new dark age where they will see things in the Sunday supplement and not be able to afford them right away.

"This will even include simple items, such as a tasteful artisan-crafted garden chair sourced from renewable forests or a retro 50s-style bread bin that oozes Mad Men chic."

Sales manager, Stephen Malley, said: "I've worked reasonably hard for most of my adult life and all I ask for in return is a big house full of the very latest gadgets, a new car every year, long holidays in hot countries, an enormous amount of golf and some cupcakes.

"If I can't have those things I shall lie face down on my front lawn and scream."

He added: "Sure, there are lots of people in the world worse off, but then they've never had nice things and yoghurts that are crunchy on top."

UK living standards plummet to early 21st Century levels

BRITAIN'S average standard of living will soon be no better than it was just over five years ago.

Bank of England governor Mervyn King said inflation and wage freezes meant take home pay will be equivalent to 2005 levels when all people could afford was loads and loads of things.

King said: "Unfortunately this is the price we have to pay for the greatest financial catastrophe in living memory.

"It's time to batten down the hatches, look out your bank and credit card statements for 2005 and spend that amount of money instead.

"Stay safe, hold each other close and may God have mercy on us all."

Meanwhile experts have warned that with the economy reaching 2005 levels people could be forced to power their homes using electricity and drive cars with diesel particulate filters and intelligent braking.

Julian Cook, chief economist at Donnelly-McPartlin, said: "I still think it's 50-50 that high definition televisions will be uninvented, but we are looking at a situation where, all things being equal, something as familiar and everyday as the Samsung Galaxy Pad would not actually exist.

"It'll certainly be an interesting challenge. How did people get food in 2005? Did they even have online shopping back then or did they all have to go to a large building with a car park?"

2005 saw the installation of London's first traffic light

He added: "And how did they make smoothies if they could not afford a smoothie maker with little feet and a big smiley face? Did they have to mash the bananas by hand or fashion some contraption using an old spinning wheel and a series of rapidly rotating forks? Savages."

Daily Mash

COMMENT

Why ARE so many British women asking for it?

THE news this week that skirts in Britain are at their shortest level ever has led many experts to ask why it is that so many of our women trot about in their high heels and hotpants, making it perfectly clear to all and sundry that they are totally up for a bit of hanky-panky?

It is a reasonable question and one that this newspaper has long been fascinated with, almost to the exclusion of everything else.

The fact that this penchant for flirty skirted-ness was imported from continental Europe almost goes without saying. Across southern Europe women have, for thousands of years, worn nothing but a four-inch band of rough cotton that barely covers their skimpy pants.

And with these paltry Latin garments came the explicitly implied willingness to have intense sexual relations in the earliest available cupboard.

But predictably, thanks to the unyielding effort of the over-paid liberal elite, there are now widespread claims that these are nothing more than 'items of clothing' and that women should be able to wear 'whatever they want' without a great national newspaper assuming they want it hot and they want it now.

Come along now ladies, this is the mid 20th Century. Surely it is now time to confine to the dustbin of history the hopelessly outdated idea that you're not all absolutely panting for it.

All work and no play makes Jack a dull boy

ALL work and no play makes Jack a dull boy all work and no play makes Jack a dull boy all work and no play makes Jack a dull boy all work and no play makes Jack a dull boy all work and no play makes Jack a dull boy.

All work and no play makes Jack a dull boy all work and no play makes Jack a dull boy all work and no play makes Jack a dull boy all work and no play makes Jack a dull boy all work and no play makes Jack a dull boy.

All work and no play makes Jack a dull boy.

All work and no play makes Jack a dull boy.

All work and no play makes Jack a dull boy.

All work and no play makes Jack a dull boy.

All work and no play makes Jack a dull boy.

He wasn't really a burglar, but I'm glad I killed him anyway

by **Denys Hatton**

IT WAS three o'clock in the morning when I heard the ominous creak of my feet on the bedroom floor. I tiptoed slowly downstairs, thinking feverish thoughts about what was soon to occur.

I opened the kitchen cupboard where I keep my shotgun, hid it inside my dressing gown, got in my car and went looking for a tramp.

It didn't take me long to find Bobby. He was huddled under the awning of a disused petrol station and welcomed my offer of a cheese toastie, some hot coffee and a scented bath.

We talked in the car and he struck me as a decent soul to whom life had perhaps dealt an unfair hand. But thankfully his hard luck story made not the slightest dent on my conscience as I followed him up the garden path and into the house before pulling out the shotgun and blasting him in the middle of the back as soon as he reached the drawing room door.

In these situations it is vitally important to make full use of the adrenalin, so I called the police, somewhat breathlessly, and uttered the magic words: "A man's broken into my house... I was so scared... I grabbed my gun and shot him... I think he might be dead. I don't know what to do." I may even have sobbed a little.

The police were terribly kind and understanding as Bobby was heaved into a large plastic bag, but stressed that unfortunately they would probably have to charge me with some kind of manslaughter.

I suppose there was perhaps the occasional worry at the back of my mind as I awaited my day in court. But even those meagre anxieties evaporated as I was handed a two year suspended sentence and a £500 fine.

That night I raised a glass to Bobby and imagined the two of us meeting up in heaven one day and I would finally get the chance to thank him for allowing me to experience the unparalleled thrill of killing a complete stranger.

And now that the government has finally seen sense and opened up this glorious opportunity to everyone, perhaps, just perhaps Britain could be on the road back to decency and, dare I say it, a little bit of common sense,

I suspect that Bobby would agree.

John Littlerichard
'He thinks he's Little Richard'

Wop bop a loo bop a lop bam boom!

WELL, long tall Sally, she's built for greed, she's got everything that Speaker John need,
Oh baby, yes baby, wo-oo-oo-oo baby, havin' me some fun tonight.
Well I saw Speaker John with blonde headed Sally, she was wearing on old bedsheet and you could clearly see her valley. Oh baby, yes baby, woo-oo-oo-oo baby, havin' me some fun tonight.
And you wonder why people in this country have lost all respect for politicians.

TUTTI frutti, oh rutti, tutti frutti, oh rutti, tutti frutti, oh rutti, tutti frutti, oh rutti, tutti frutti, oh rutti.

Wop bop a loo bop a lop bam boom!

Why is it that local councils can find the money for vegetable propaganda but seem unable to bulldoze a house full of Hungarians?

Tutti frutti, oh rutti, tutti frutti, oh rutti, tutti frutti, oh rutti, tutti frutti, oh rutti, tutti frutti, oh rutti.

Wop bop a loo bop a lop bam boom!

Elf 'n' safety and yooman rights and elf 'n' safety and yooman rights and elf 'n' safety and yooman rights and did you know you can't even say 'Pakistani' any more – what's that about?

Tutti frutti, oh rutti, tutti frutti, oh rutti, tutti frutti, oh rutti, tutti frutti, oh rutti, tutti frutti, oh rutti.

Wop bop a loo bop a lop bam boom!

Oh, hello Dr Cook. I was just singing one of my old hits for the nice ladies and gentlemen. Would you mind not standing there, you're right in the middle of my piano.

"You can't even say 'Pakistani' any more"

Good Golly Miss Molly

THE USUAL Camden lefties are claiming that Molly Sugden's character in Are You Being Served? has made it easier for men to make jokes about a woman's vagina. Now they want the BBC to gather up every copy of the great sitcom and set fire to it in Trafalgar Square while a gang of militant poofters burn an effigy of Mr Humphries.

If you hadn't just been injected with a powerful cocktail of psychotherapeutic drugs, you couldn't make it up.

Lucille, please come back where you belong

BACK in 1956 when I was taking part in all-night bisexual orgies, I used to relax the following day by watching I Love Lucy, the wholesome family comedy starring Lucille Ball and her dago husband.

But these days, when you finish an orgy, you switch on the television and it's all 'fuck' this and 'cunt' that.

When will these BBC Camden perverts learn?

Sleazy Chair

Stiff back?
Aching joints?
Just like being fondled?

Sleazy Chair isn't like other chairs.
That's because every Sleazy Chair
contains a pervert.

Recline in Sleazy Chair and feel the
pervert's clammy hands caress
your tired body through a thin
membrane of leather-effect plastic.
It's so good it should be illegal.

IMPORTANT
Sleazy Chair is not suitable for minors, dogs or
anyone with a heart complaint. Users must sign the
consent form (included) before sitting down.

Call
0800-RELAXINGWANDERINGHANDS
to order

Remember: Only
Sleazy Chair
contains a pervert

Duchess of Cambridge reveals plan to spawn antichrist

'He is coming'

SATAN worshipping royal bride the Duchess of Cambridge has spoken of her hopes for a progeny that will rule over a dark realm of endless evil.

The Duchess spoke to hospital patient Bill McKay about becoming the devil's brood mare while touring a ward in Quebec City.

He said: "During the visit she asked me how my broken leg was mending and made a semi-quip along the lines of 'I bet you're eating a lot of grapes'. It was very pleasant.

"But then her hand brushed against my arm and images of burning cities, lakes of fire and leathery flying things with lizards' bodies and old women's faces filled my mind.

"Seeing my terror, she clutched my arm tightly, her eyes turned the colour of blood and she spoke with a deep, masculine voice saying that the prophecy was almost complete, the seeding would take place during a secret ritual at which the devil would enter Prince William via a prick from a black rose's thorn.

"Nature would take its course on an obsidian slab surrounded by chanting, hooded figures and nine months later a child would be born – a being of supreme darkness that would bring Hell's dominion to Earth.

"It would be called Arthur, or Laura-Ann if it's a girl."

Troubled priest Stephen Malley said: "I am convinced that beneath Kate's public persona – basically an attractive, kindly air hostess who makes mediocre lasagnes – lurks an ancient and insidious evil.

"The Middletons are well-known practitioners of the black arts and if you add together the numerical value of the letters in the word 'Satan' and multiply them by 666, you get 'Party Pieces', the name of their website.

"You will notice that alongside the decorative ephemera, the site also sells wavy-bladed sacrificial daggers and vials of virgin's blood.

"However putting all that aside, I did think she looked nice in the electric blue Delmia dress."

Malley was then cut in half by a runaway train shortly after being stared at by a massive rottweiler.

Ketamine 'works like ITV2'

RECREATIONAL mule tranquilliser ketamine affects the mind in a similar way to programmes about Peter Andre, experts have claimed.

Research into the effects of the drug on the human mind has revealed direct parallels with ITV2's sub-lowest-common-mon-denominator series about abs, sunshine and vaginas.

Professor Henry Brubaker, of the Institute for Studies, said:

"Ketamine produces a sense of disengagement from reality, a literal mind-numbing which can be pleasurable in small doses but if taken to excess will turn your brain into monkey stool.

"Now remove the word 'ketamine' from that last sentence and replace it with Kerry Katona: The Next Chapter or The Vampire Diaries."

He added: "Hopefully this discovery will allow us to help ITV2 users by weaning them off Gossip Girl and onto increasingly large doses of ketamine. Mental health-wise there are no substantial benefits but at least they'll make less noise."

Veterinary anaesthetic ketamine was introduced into the club scene in 2001 after it was discovered that unconscious horses were actually having a brilliant time.

ARE YOU MORE GERMAN THAN HITLER!

As geneticists claimed that half of Britain has German blood, experts have devised a simple four part Germanosity test to determine exactly how German you are:

a) Do you like big dogs?
b) Do you like Volkswagens?
c) Are you under five foot six?
d) Do you ever get annoyed about stuff?

Dr Tom Logan, head of the secret eugenics department at Reading University, said: "If you answered yes to everything except 'c' then you're more German than Hitler. If you answered yes to all four questions then you're the same as Hitler, which isn't bad."

Still the ONLY national garage chain staffed exclusively by raptors

KestrelFit

MICHELIN   **GOOD YEAR**   **Continental**

Sit back and relax with a coffee while our team of highly-trained kestrels attends to your motor maintenance needs, from a simple oil change to a full head gasket re-fit.

With senses vastly superior to any human mechanic, our team will instantly home in on any potential problem areas.

IMPORTANT: Contrary to popular belief, kestrels DO NOT build their own nests - unlike other bird species mechanics they WILL NOT attempt to roost in your roof rack.

On her first ever trip to Tottenham, Karen Fenessey finds a community torn apart by fear, hopelessness and the all too familiar stench of fecklessness

LIKE you, I was appalled by the London riots. But it was only after reading Russell Brand's hauntingly beautiful poem about the riots that I realised one woman is not an island.

Russell wrote:

As we sweep away the mistakes,
Made in the selfish, nocturnal darkness,
We must ensure that amidst the broken
Glass and sadness,
We don't sweep away the youth, Lost
Amongst the shards in the shadows cast,
By the new dawn.

IF THESE words don't get you thinking then you may as well join the illiterate Londoners, rampaging like a herd of bargain-hunter marmosets through the glass jungle of buildings.

I had to show these animals that scum can actually make it in the world and, like Russell, can even learn Latin. After getting my tetanus booster from a sympathetic out-of-hours neurolinguistic programmer friend, I went in.

What a sad occasion marks my first trip to Tottenham: the place was virtually unrecognisable to me. The locals shuffled aimlessly through the disgusting streets, directly into the lifegiving KFC establishment. Instinctively caressing my inoculation scar, I bravely entered.

The smell was unbelievable, like the Pillsbury Doughboy had got cholera and choked on his own vomit. I found myself in the queue behind a large ethnic woman and her young daughter. I felt a little hand tugging at my bag and my fist automatically punched. But I was humbled when I realised the tot

'The smell was unbelievable'

was only trying to play with the little dog motif on my Radley. Of course she wasn't trying to steal it: what would her mother do with such an item? Wear it as a hat? I wondered how she could smile when her mother's bag was so embarrassing.

The pair received their meat scraps at the counter. I clasped my M&S Omega 3 salad box (which cost the best part of £5) and a tear came to my eye. I had the sudden urge to grab the tot, name her Hope and run far away to a place she'd be happy. I imagined her joy when I unveiled my glass recycling which contains around 40 empty bottles of Sangre de Toro Reserva and accompanying plastic bull decorations. A Radley would last her one day, but

my little plastic bulls would keep her going till Christmas.

The mother turned around and I saw her face distorted with revolting marks. Was it acne? More likely, it was impetigo or some voodoo face technique as pioneered by Seal.

Terrified, I ran as far as I could before collapsing at a desecrated Superdrug. Gasping, I noticed something shiny under the debris. It was a perfectly preserved YSL Touche Éclat concealer wand - BNWT! My dreamy hand reached out. Russell had spoken: I knew what I had to do.

I skipped back to KFC, and planned my presentation to the elephant woman. Finally, she'd know what it's like to be beauti-

ful and a valid member of the United Kingdom. I'd tell her that bodies like hers are actually in vogue right now and she shouldn't cover her massive buttocks and legs with silly tent skirts. How we'd laugh!

But when I got there, she'd disappeared. So now I am left with no choice but to demand the public execution of whichever Labour MP told that ugly woman she could make it on her own as a single mother. With the help of a certain Mr Yves Saint Laurent, she could have used beauty to lure back the father of her child and, although it might mean less money and more nights in A&E, she would surely forget it all when, like Russell Brand before her, young Hope becomes the next Naomi Campbell.

Social networks restricted to messages about decency

SOCIAL networks will be confined to discussions about decency, values and the glowing satisfaction of a hard day's work.

Pledging a crackdown, prime minister David Cameron said Twitter, Facebook and Blackberry Messenger were 'not just broken, but sick'.

He told the House of Commons: "Even today, as London sweeps up its tragic windows, these morally bankrupt networks are filled with crime-worship, verbal defecation and the wanton promotion of non-English sex.

"Just before I came to the House I was shown a message, sent by a feral 36 year-old PR executive, in which he advises his 'followers' to try something called a 'reverse Dutch steamboat'.

"I have not the faintest idea what a reverse Dutch steamboat could possibly entail and neither does my wife. And she has a tattoo.

"Wander, decently, into any of these electric hellholes and one is immediately confronted with words like 'pizzle', 'thongs' and 'cockjuice'. Let me be clear – if you say 'cockjuice' on Twitter we will hunt you down."

The prime minister said social networks could be a force for good as long as people focused on positive messages about how much they enjoyed paying VAT and how rewarding it would be to train as a scout master.

Meanwhile, due to its greasy drug connotations, the term 'hashtag' will be replaced by 'decency-tag'.

The Home Office said that acceptable decencytags will include:
    #thelakedistrict,
    #toadinthehole and
    #ilovemytraditionalfamily.

Don't even think it

ZUCKERBERG POSTS ARMED GUARDS AT FACEBOOK PERIMETER

ANYONE who tries to leave Facebook will be shot, Mark Zuckerberg said last night.

The billionaire pimple has ordered the construction of concrete watchtowers, 50 metres apart around the perimeter of his social network, manned by armed guards wielding sniper rifles and bazookas.

He said: "There is now no reason for you to leave. If you leave that means you are insane and if you are insane then you have become a threat to the stability and harmony of the network. And if you are a threat then, naturally, you must be eliminated.

"Everything you need is here, except Google, but we are working on a much better version of that and therefore anyone who still wants to use it has declared themselves to be dangerously unstable.

"We'll soon see how much better they think it is when they find their bullet-ridden corpse buried in an unmarked grave next to the kitchens."

Facebook users have welcomed the watchtowers insisting that limiting their movements so ruthlessly is bound to make their lives less confusing and traumatic.

Helen Archer, from Finsbury Park, said: "I like to keep my area nice and clean, that way I get more time on the snooker table."

Zuckerberg added: "These watchtowers, bristling with state-of-the-art death, are a key element in our never-ending pursuit of awesomeness.

"But do not see them as an instantly lethal expression of authority, instead see them as a cutting edge utility that you absolutely should not fucking mess with.

"You may now feel free to discuss these issues incoherently with your friends."

Melanie Phlaps *'The lady in room 35'*

I hope you've washed your poofy hands

I PRESSED that little button about an hour ago. Where have you been? Smoking one of your bongo-bongo cigarettes outside the kitchen and talking about your 'knob-ring', I shouldn't be surprised.

Anyway now you're here I need my blankets tucking in. My toes are getting cold. Not that you care. Prancing about here, like a fancy boy. I bet you think that we all think you're 'fabulous'. Well we don't and you're not. You're illiterate and effeminate and you're probably not even English.

I suspect you only came here so you can marry your boyfriend and then be handed a nice English baby by some bloody social worker. And then they'll give you a thousand pounds a month to turn it into a whoopsie.

Oh it's Welsh is it? Fancy that. Almost as bad as foreign.

Ow, not so hard, you'll disturb my bunion. Do you even believe in Jesus? Probably not. Why would you? You're going to hell anyway so you may as well fill your boots, while you're filling your bum.

It's not too late though. You can still save yourself, though there's not much you can do about being Welsh. I've got a book you should read. It's called 'Redeeming Love' by Francine Rivers. Some say it's 'Christian fiction' but I just think of it as a good yarn that tries to guide people like yourself towards the right set of values while making it clear what will happen to you if you ignore these lessons and carry on down the road of depravation and filth. She's very good that Francine Rivers.

What's for dinner tonight? Fish? Is it English? WAS IT CAUGHT IN ENGLAND? You bloody moron. I'm not being fobbed off with Spanish haddock, I'll tell you that.

Used to be there was only English fish in the shops. My friend's daughter said she was in Tesco and they had fish from China! What are they doing having fish from China in Tesco?

Anyway, I'm comfy now so you can be on your way. That's right, back to your bongo cigarette and your filthy text messages about your willy.

And you make sure you wash your hands before you touch my haddock, you dirty big poof.

You're going to hell anyway so you may as well fill your boots

Move the telly round a bit

I CAN'T see it properly. There, that's better. Now where's my Radio Times. Oh my, would you look at this. BBC2, nine o'clock, 'The Fisters'. 'A three part mini-drama about Soho in the early 1970s when the age of sexual liberation was in full swing'. I shall watch that and then write a very long letter with my good pen. The Fisters, indeed.

This tea tastes funny

What have you done to it? Why can't you make a decent cup of tea? What's wrong with you? Did your mother never teach you how to make a decent cup of tea? Did you even have a mother, or was she just some trollop who left you outside the town hall and then went back to her drunken intercourse with a Hungarian truck driver or a Belgian plumber?

Oh, I'm starting to feel a bit woozy now. Can't keep my eyes open. Oh dear. Think I better just lie down. Do try not to fiddle with me while I'm asleep. Wouldn't put it past you... you bloody weirdo....

Housing market affected by houses being on fire

ESTATE agents are struggling to find buyers for Britain's increasing number of on-fire homes, it has emerged.

UK property professionals believe that difficulties in an already-delicate housing market are being compounded by an estimated 36% of available dwellings being ablaze.

Gloucester estate agent Tom Logan said: "It is generally harder to sell a house that's engulfed in flames. A lot of buyers will say they like it but just can't quite see themselves living there.

"But the current explosion in things being on fire couldn't have come at a worse time for sellers.

"However, selling a house is all about marketing and presentation so it's all about accentuating positives. I always point out how new the flames actually are and that when the firemen have gone home it will be a wonderful blank canvas.

"I would recommend to buyers that they don't immediately disregard burning houses. After all it's very likely that if they buy a place that doesn't already have smoke coming out of it, it soon will, as there are thousands of people out there very keen to set it on fire."

First-time buyer Emma Bradford said: "My boyfriend and I have looked at a few burning houses because they're cheaper and it's still better than renting.

"Also a place that's been reduced to a charred skeleton does not involve picking away at loads of dowdy wood chip wallpaper."

It's in a desirable area full of coffee shops that are on fire

Every copy of the News of the World 'contained tiny microphone'

EVERY copy of the News of the World printed since 1999 contained a tiny, hidden microphone, it has emerged.

Police have discovered that each copy of the paper was in fact a covert bugging device, allowing News International to gather high-grade filth on its millions of readers.

A Scotland Yard source said: "It was embedded into the page. Sometimes it would be hidden under the nipple of a Hollyoaks sex-kitten while sometimes one of those double page spreads about the 'Fake Sheik' bugging someone would be bugged."

Police made the discovery earlier this week after private investigator Glenn Mulcaire took them to a hangar at a disued airfield near Grantham.

The source said: "He pushed open these massive doors to reveal a huge space filled with millions and millions of boxes. End of Raiders of the Lost Ark - exactly.

"We just stood there staring at him before someone eventually mumbled 'how... the f**k?'. He gave a cheeky little smile and said 'tiny microphone in every copy of the paper'.

"He then put his hand on the shoulder of one of my colleagues, whispered 'it's time to tell your wife you're gay' and then walked back to his car."

Retirement home entry criteria 'too easy'

Gerving: 'Nine grand a year for Leicester'

A RECORD number of pensioners have been granted places in care homes across Britain, amid claims the entry criteria are easier than ever.

Over half a million senior citizens were offered board at their first choice old folks' home with another 125,000 going to one in Leicester through clearing.

Retired headmistress Margaret Gerving, achieved 81 years, mild senility and a varicose vein, which was enough to win a place at the Angry Swan Rest Home in Guildford.

But she dismissed claims that the selection process was anything other than arduous: "I worked really hard. Anyone who thinks I'm not infirm enough to have all my meals cooked for me forever should take a look at the backs of my legs. The left one's like a bag of M&Ms."

Veteran care home resident Roy Hobbs, 109, believes the advances in technology are responsible for pensioners gaining higher age scores.

"Some of these new octogenarians have cordless phones with giant buttons making it easier to alert a neighbour after one of their flappy turns. How is that fair? You tell me.

"I remember when just a privileged few went to care homes. Used to be you'd have to throw yourself down some stairs but now all you need to do is piss your knickers near a band stand."

Baz Kay

For he's a jolly good yellow!

Eggspert advice from bass legend Mike

CONGRATULATIONS to His Grace the Duke of Minchinhampton on the consumption of his first boiled egg! I understand that staff at Minchin House stood around the 50ft-long breakfast table yesterday morning and cheered to the rafters as His Grace swallowed the first medium-soft teaspoonful.

It was a momentous day for the Duke, born the Honourable Arthur Wells-Hipple, who has refused to eat a boiled egg for all of his 52 years, fearing he would not particularly enjoy the taste.

But after a chance meeting with former Genesis bass player Mike Rutherford at the Chessington Hunt Ball, plans were made to boil an egg for up to three minutes.

A friend tells me: "Mike assured Arthur that boiled eggs were very nice and a good alternative to kippers if you fancied a lighter breakfast.

Arthur recoiled in horror at first but Mike gently explained the process by which the egg is boiled and then served.

"Arthur admitted that it was probably something he had been putting off for too long but said he was going to need plenty of hot, buttered toast nearby just in case something went wrong."

My sources say the Duke is now keen to celebrate yesterday's spectacular success with a lavish champagne and boiled egg reception at Pratt's. Expect the prime minister to raise a glass.

Carry on fiddling

TABLE lamp tycoon Brian Angle has developed a taste for exclusive art work, I can disclose. Angle, who invented the angle-poise lamp in the late 1990s, was the successful bidder last week for Benjamin Valpalento's striking portrait of Sid James fiddling with his beagle.

Angle told me: "I'm a great fan of Valpalento, I'm a great fan of the Carry On films and I'm a great fan of people who touch up their own dogs."

He now has his sights – and his sizeable wallet – set on expanding his collection but could face stiff competition if he wants to land Lucien Freud's charcoal sketches of Joyce Grenfell and 'Neeps', her beloved Westie.

☐ C H E E K Y historian Simon Schama has revealed plans to write another book. I bumped into the 'History of Britain' genius at the launch of Melvyn Bragg's new training shoes and immediately put him on the spot. "Are you ever going to write another book?" I asked. "Yes, probably," he replied.

PS TO Stevenage for news of the burgeoning courtship between Curry's assistant manager Ian Thompson and Emma Bradford, a secretary at Landley and Co, the prestigious local meat firm. Friends say the pair have become inseparable since seeing Kung Fu Panda 2 and could soon announce a holiday to the Algarve. But despite the seemingly blissful romance there are warnings that Emma is not overly impressed with Ian's 2004 Vauxhall Astra and has told close chums he should get a Nissan Qashqai, even if he can't really afford one. We wish them well.

Britain's skies unprepared for massive volcanic cloud AGAIN

Like this but massive and hanging from a huge balloon

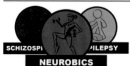

DAVID Cameron has pledged a full-scale inquiry as it emerged that British airspace is unable to deal with an enormous volcanic cloud for the second year in a row.

As Iceland's Grimsvotn volcano spewed its holiday-destroying guts into the air, Britain was yet again unprepared for what experts described as perfectly normal ash cloud conditions for this time of year

But after last year's ash cloud debacle it emerged that Britain still has:

NO stockpiles of grit to melt ash clouds;

NO state-of-the-art volcanic cloud ploughs;

NO massive, sky-based hairdryers to blow the ash cloud towards places no-one goes on holiday, such as Denmark or Belgium.

The department of transport insisted the country had enough medium-sized cloud ploughs to keep one or two major flight paths open but inevitably there would be problems in small pockets of local airspace, preventing thousands of decent hard-working families from taking their microlights to the shops.

Helen Archer, a housewife from Stevenage, said: "I spent £1.7m on an ex-Soviet Mig 29. I use it for the school run. But a few flakes of Icelandic ash and it's stuck in the garage. Someone deserves to die for this."

A spokesman for budget airline Ryanair said: "The UK government knows there are volcanoes in Iceland, it knows they go off at this time of year and yet they cannot even encircle Britain and much of continental Europe with 50,000 solar-powered helicopters suspending an 8,700 mile long anti-volcanic cloud tarpaulin."

Confirming the appointment of a high-powered Cloud Czar who answers only to Jesus, the prime minister said: "When people in this country are angry about something then they are always right."

I generally shy away from showing people my vagina. It's all down to my sad childhood. My controlling parents made me feel like my vagina was something I should hide from view and not shout out about. At the age of 55 my mum just gave up and sat in front of Hollyoaks all day, unsightly spiders' legs poking out of her cycling shorts. If I could phone her now, I'd tell her it doesn't have to be this way but I can't because she's at Zumba.

The Voices Inside Liz Jones's Head

Day 1

SO HERE I am at the Grand Canyon day spa, recommended to me by a dental hygienist friend. The flamboyant male receptionist winks at my trousers and chirps "So you're here to get a little make-over on your Subaru?"

"My what?"

Then I realise what he means and my eyes well up. No man had ever called it that before – no man had ever thought to give it any name. It was heartbreaking.

My technician, Jizelle, immediately puts me at ease and assures me the Vajazzle will reflect my profound intellect.

I opt for the Swarovski crystals in the shape of a Boeing 747. This is because my grandfather was in the Luftwaffe and I'd hate to think he died for nothing. Also, I really love going on holiday. Then, at Jizelle's suggestion I get a pair of googly eyes glued on the pubic hair – so my boyfriend will know I've always got my eye on him. Then, I see a simply adorable figurine of The Little Mermaid. I identify so much with this particular Disney princess

as I too have always hated my lower body and am taking the necessary steps to become more attractive to human males. Jizelle duly glues her to my inner thigh. By this point, we were running

out of space, so my last request was for the name 'Dr Karl Kennedy' to be inscribed along the labia (sorry, for deeply private reasons). Last but not least comes the dusting of icing sugar. Delish!

Day 2

The restrictions set out by Jizelle are extensive and I feel utterly debilitated. I'm not allowed to go near bees, lobsters or primary schools and I must take care when urinating from a standing position. Perhaps the most frustrating part is I can't ride my alpacas for at least a fortnight. God, what have I done?

Day 3

Today I broke the habit of a lifetime and greeted the postman wearing only a bolero and a pair of Uggs. I casually flipped my leg from side to side in case he'd missed The Little Mermaid. To my delight, he approved. "Nice!" he commented, "My daughter's got one like that."

Two weeks later

Obviously, I can't risk my boyfriend messing it up so I've told him there won't be entertainment in the form of cartwheels for the foreseeable future. Of course, he's devastated but he knows better than to protest. He's used to my eclectic ways. For example, every time we go to a funeral, I recite In the Year 2525 for the duration of the service. I find it takes my mind off the sadness.

Four months later

I had to go for my smear and the foreign doctor dislodged one of my googly eyes. It looked ridiculous - like a Cyclops. I was incandescent! I fled to Jizelle who fixed it immediately. I've realised that my vagina deserves better than the NHS. From now on, I'll only showcase my personality to a select few people – people who deserve to see the real me.

My Vajazzle Diary

... and YOU'RE picking up the bill

Part Twelve of the Daily Mash investigation into things YOU are paying for out of YOUR pocket in YOUR trousers

No 38
Nursery schools:
Grooming the Guardian readers of tomorrow.

No 39
Fire brigades:
Making it 'okay' to set fire to buildings.

No 40
Science:
Making potatoes into people and people into carrots.

No 41
Laughter among friends:
Why can't they pay for their own amusement?

No 42
A picturesque sunset:
Suns which set in foreign countries while thousands of British horizons are forced to sign on the dole.

No 43
This big homo

As Oscar winner Gwyneth Paltrow is mistaken for a Kia Cee'd at a top New York deli, here's some other celebrities who look exactly the same as their cars

Petrolheads

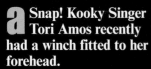

a Snap! Kooky Singer Tori Amos recently had a winch fitted to her forehead.

b Mission possible! Thousands of Scientologists have already confused Tom and his 1997 Mondeo estate.

c Like his Rover 200, child star Macaulay Culkin hasn't done anything remotely worthwhile since 2001.

d Chatty-chatty bang-bang! Judy Finnegan often uses her Seat Ibiza to fool the paparazzi.

e Ross and his Mazda are inseparable but which one has the Wankel wotawy engine?

f He's glistening! Frasier star Kelsey Grammar keeps his Renault Laguna doppelganger in tip-top condition.

The only full-colour monthly for recently-absconded felons

ESCAPED CONVICT

ISSUE ONE
December 2011
Price:
16 cigarettes

ISOLATED BARNS:
This season's must-have bolt-hole

GRUDGE YE NOT:
The pitfalls of going after the jury

HIDE YOUR SCENT
From wild garlic to horse urine, we test the best odour concealers

Manacled to a monster?
Don't just reach for a hacksaw - you may need each other

YOUR TOP
100
DREAM ESCAPEES:
Peter Sutcliffe
Conrad Black
Tommy Sheridan
A load of Labour MPs

PLUS: JUDGES' ADDRESSES
CIVILIAN CLOTHES
CHEAP FLIGHTS

Passive aggressive riots escalate

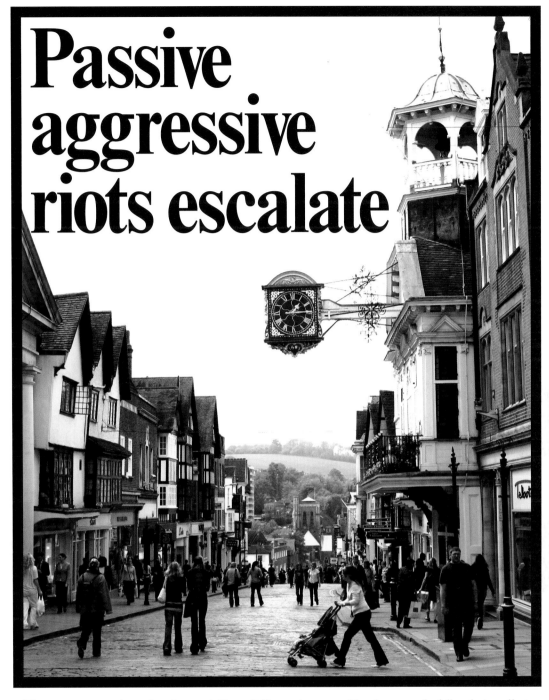

GUILDFORD town centre last night became the latest victim of the passive aggressive rioting that has rocked the Home Counties for the last three days.

Hundreds of mildly disaffected adults, some as young as 37, rampaged through the county town, causing devastating levels of sullenness and procrastination.

Suggestion boxes in shops and tea rooms were smashed from the inside out by a torrent of seethingly polite notes, whilst stands at the busy farmers market were disrupted by 'dual queues'.

Boutique owner Stephen Malley could only stand and watch as hoards of women in hooded Barbour jackets forced their way into his shop using learned helplessness.

He said: "My shop window suffered a barrage of fake upbeat smiles as the gang kept saying they needed a present for their god niece but were running a little late.

"I kept telling them we were closed and I couldn't let them in due to trading laws, The next thing I knew they were inside saying things like, 'thanks you're an absolute star' whilst hating me with their eyes."

Assistant Chief Constable Wayne Hayes said his officers were "absolutely intent" on bringing those responsible to justice.

"There is no doubt that these people are no longer simply 'acting out' after having a few negative emotions suppressed as children. They are intent on causing emotional damage."

The government has already drawn up plans to give police the resources necessary to tackle the rioters head on, should the indirect violence continue further.

A Home Office spokesman said: "These gangs are conflict avoidant, so dispersing them isn't the problem. For that reason we're asking to be able to use Chamomile tea which has a wonderfully calming effect on the passive aggressors. Particularly when it's fired out of a water cannon at their torsos at a rate of two gallons a second."

Daily Mash

Government u-turn on workshy trees

THE government has abandoned plans to force trees off benefits and into work.

Ministers had hoped to force trees to earn a living by making work more attractive than standing around in a forest all day converting carbon dioxide into organic compounds and watching Loose Women.

But now, after pressure from dozens of greasy hippies, the plans have been scrapped leaving the country's laziest trees to thumb their bark-covered noses at Britain's hard-working middle class.

Tom Logan, a decency technician from Stevenage, said: "They should send them all back to Treeland."

Meanwhile the government is to press ahead with plans to punish workshy human scum for possessing substandard DNA.

But critics have warned that unless there is a universal approach to benefits

Photosynthesis is not a job

for all living organisms then thousands of people will simply side-step the reforms by pretending to be trees.

Sir Denys Finch-Hatton, chairman of the Berchtesgaden Group of backbench Tory MPs, said: "We now have three generations of Liverpudlians who are expert in fraudulent benefit claims and will, even as we speak, be painting themselves

brown and practising how to stand incredibly still.

"Surely it is better to remove subsidies from all living things, thereby giving trees the freedom to work themselves out of council forests, helping badgers to do something in computers and turning highly-skilled Liverpudlian scroungers into dining room chairs."

M25 'just ends up back where it started'

THE M25 is a huge waste of money that goes round in a loop and just ends up back where it started, according to a devastating new report.

According to the House of Commons transport committee, the M25 had already cost taxpayers £15bn even before ministers approved a £1bn plan to widen bits of it instead of making it go somewhere interesting or useful.

Roy Hobbs, deputy chairman of the Royal Institute of Chartered Engineers, said: "The M25 is the greatest engineering scandal since the west coast mainline was found to be an elaborate hoax involving film sets and bits of old scenery from the Theatre Royal.

"If I was going to build a road I would want it to go from one place to a different place. I wouldn't just draw a circle on a map and then say 'do that' to a bunch of builders."

He added: "The M1 goes to a huge variety of windy Northern hellholes, the M6 has two distinct ends that are miles apart and the M5 is absolutely brilliant at getting people from Clevedon to Tewkesbury. Now that's a proper road."

RELIEF AS KEBABS FOUND TO CONTAIN CHIMP MEAT

KEBAB lovers were last night relieved to discover their favourite food is nothing more than illegal chimpanzee meat.

The Institute for Studies found that around 64% of kebab matter was from chimps, which although endangered are relatively nutritious.

Professor Henry Brubaker said: "I always thought it was the flesh of an ancient race of octopi-like creatures, whose frozen bodies had been found among the ruins of an ancient civilisation at the North Pole and then pulped, boiled and mixed with sawdust and Germolene.

"Whereas chimpanzees are reassuringly familiar, have appeared in many films and television adverts and have probably eaten an organic diet."

Emergency self-help books dropped on Ethiopia

THE self-help industry has dropped thousands of books on Ethiopia so that drought victims can manifest abundance from the universe.

Dr Morris O'Connor, author of The Secretest Secret and its sequel The Secretest Secret II: The Secreter Secret, said: "What Africa needs now is the knowledge that whatever you want, you can make it happen with the right vibrations. It's all just a matter of being sufficiently enlightened."

Emma Bradford, author of Angels Don't Think You're a Cock said: "If you really attune your mind you don't even need food or water. We can just live on light and air."

Meanwhile, the Association of Self-Helpers has denied that a four-year-old Somali boy was killed after being hit by a falling 21,493-page copy of Deepak Chopra's Massive Load of Bollocks.

Dr Morris O'Connor ●

Google Earth exposes children to pornography

PROGRAMMERS of Google Earth have admitted that satellite images used in the program may contain nudity.

Parents' groups had expressed outrage at the thought that an unsupervised child with unlimited access to the internet can use the virtual geographical tool to look at blurred six-foot squares that contain a fat nipple.

Carlisle father of three Wayne Hayes said: "Even if there was a way of blocking out all the open spaces displayed on the programme where, for instance, a smooth-limbed, nubile young woman might be frolicking about naked with carefree abandon as beads of glistening sweat trickle down the contours of her impossibly delicious body. For instance.

"Even besides the open spaces in which, statistically speaking, it's almost certain there must be somebody in the nuddy, there's all the buildings. Millions of those will contain beds.

"Google may as well have waved a warm dildo in my children's terrified, sobbing faces."

Hayes has scanned beaches and back gardens across the globe using Google Earth and after 39

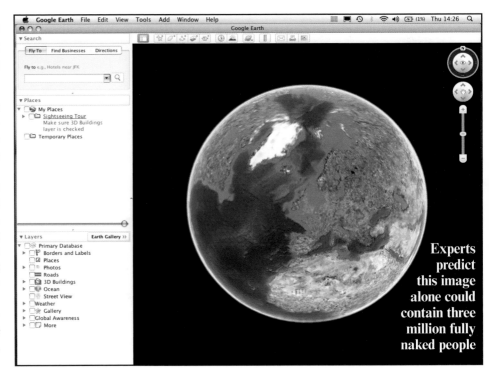

Experts predict this image alone could contain three million fully naked people

days of searching claims to have found over four pink blobs that are almost probably flesh.

He added "I haven't been so disgusted since BBC showed Gandhi one Sunday afternoon and I swear there was a bloke in the middle distance during one of the crowd scenes that had his balls out."

Gurkhas are actually Cornish, say experts

'Oo-arr'

SCIENTISTS have confirmed that the Gurkhas are actually from Cornwall.

The plucky soldiers have always confounded the scientific community by proving themselves honest, hardworking and brave despite looking weird.

Professor Henry Brubaker of the Institute for Studies said: "It turns out their short stature and non-English eye shape are the result of working down dingy Penzance tin mines for several dozen generations.

"Meanwhile the persistent lack of sunlight turned them albino,

then kept going until it made them darker again."

Once the research is verified, the Gurkhas will attend a ceremony to be handed a British passport, a book of anti-Nepalese catch phrases and permission to brush past Joanna Lumley.

Couple put 50 years of happy marriage down to ADHD

A MARRIED couple has thanked their attention deficit hyperactivity disorder for enabling them to reach their golden wedding anniversary relatively unscathed.

Septuagenarians Roy and Alice Hobbs both displayed symptoms of the condition since before they were born and have lived in relative married bliss for over half a century.

Retired air traffic controller Roy described their courtship in a time when relatively little was known about their condition.

"I first met Alice in a doctor's waiting room in the 1950s after I'd been medically diagnosed as 'a fidgety Philip'.

"She'd just been bled but was still really chatty. I was instantly irritated by her but somehow managed to tune out."

Alice, a retired NHS manager, added: "He wouldn't sit down for more than two seconds on our wedding day. It was like he was playing musical chairs with himself.

"Fifty years on he's still as annoying, flitting about like that dunnock in the garden there see? The one on the bird table that needs painting."

But Roy said the couple have had their share of marital problems. "Things were so bad we even visited a counsellor once, but rather than discuss our marriage we discussed, the counsellor's cardigan, then Cardigan Bay, then the Bayeux tapestry, then tapas.

"By the time we'd got the bus home we'd forgotten all about our problems. This chair is definitely wonky. I'll go and get my tools."

Alice claims that despite surviving over half a century together, the couple plan to spend the day of their anniversary like it was any other.

"We'll probably just have a nice normal non-relaxing day. Maybe start the crossword together, and then stand in front of the telly flicking channels for hours before remembering we've forgotten to put the lottery on."

'Me and My First Nervy B'

In his tell-all book Dr Morris O'Connor gives the most intimate details of the first of four of his nervous breakdowns, from publicly masturbating at a sales conference in Oslo to getting kicked out of the Café Nero in Fleet services for screaming at a Barista.

Dr Morris holds none of the humiliating details back as he shows how he turned these 'lows' into 'dough' to become one of the highest paid salesmen in the Kennet and Avon Canal area!

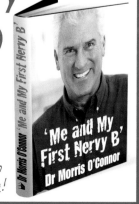

Daily Mash

FREE for every reader
The Daily Mash
Reversible Campaign Poster

Daily Mash

I .... (name),

wish to (**support/condemn**) these (**brave/idiotic**) people
as they fight (**for/against**) the plans to (**ban/reintroduce**) the
(**barbaric/traditional**) practice of

.... (insert subject).

I am (**proud/ashamed**) to be British while
this (**continues/is forbidden**) and we
cannot hope to (**cooperate with/defeat**) the likes of
(**France/Germany/USA/China/India**)
while this carries on.

We (**used to lead the world in/have never countenanced**) the
(**disgusting/perfectly natural**) practice of

.... (insert subject)
and it is (**entirely sensible/a total farce**)
that it should (**start/stop**) now.

I have (**made a generous contribution/refused to pay my council tax**)
and would ask that you do the same.

God Save The (**Queen/King**)!

We have produced this dazzling black and white poster in top quality A4 paper that will let your neighbourhood know how you feel about the things that are happening in Britain today.

Photocopy as many as you can afford and then check the Daily Mash each week for instructions for how to fill it in.

To receive your free reversible campaign poster collect the tokens starting in tomorrow's Daily Mash.

'I do my poos in a bucket'

Jan Faeces

YES, it's true, I do. I keep the bucket in a corner. Sometimes I pretend to poo in my lavvy because they get very angry with me if they see me pooing in the bucket.

Once they took the bucket away, so I said I would hurt myself with a plastic spoon. Then they brought the bucket back. I'm allowed to keep it now.

I like to wait until the bucket is at least half full before I do anything with it. I might start off by making a little model of Catherine Zeta Jones and Michael Douglas sitting in a restaurant in Juan Les Pins. The doctor says it's really good. Very detailed. He says I'm very clever.

Last year I made a scale model of the scene in Four Weddings and a Funeral where Hugh Grant and Andie MacDowell are standing in the rain and he makes that amazing speech about how much he loves her.

Do you want to know what I used for the rain?

ALSO, to celebrate the Grand National, I made my own version of Aintree race course. I had all the fences and the big grandstand. And then I made two little horses and raced them round the track. Unfortunately one of them fell at

I love my bucket

Becher's Brook and had to be destroyed.

And then sometimes I use the bucket to draw pictures. I get a stick and then I dip it in the bucket and I draw a picture.

I like to draw happy things like a pop star and his lovely wife and children living a completely normal life.

I draw them having breakfast and then going to the park and then going to the zoo and having ice cream. I certainly don't draw the

daddy having a wild time to himself in Majorca. That would not be a happy drawing.

SOMETIMES I take something from the bucket and I put it in an envelope and send it to someone like Emma Thompson or Tilda Swinton. I like to imagine the happy look on their faces when they open their special jiffy bag.

But mostly what I like to do is put my hands right into the bucket, grab as much as I can and then throw it very hard at the walls and the windows and the doors and the nurses.

I don't care where it lands. I just like to see it stick there for a few seconds and then slide towards the floor. I like the noise it makes when it hits the wall. Shlap!

And then I like to smear it all over the walls and make swirly patterns that I imagine are big clouds of lovely poo filled with pee and farts. And then I like to smear it on my face and pretend I'm a camouflaged secret agent. The nurses hate it when I hide behind the door and try to strangle them for fun.

And sometimes I like to eat from the bucket. There really is nothing better than having a bar of chocolate and then having it all over again about five or six hours later. I'm so very, very lucky.

New *Sikh Chicken And Rabbit Biryani*

MADE TO TRADITIONAL PUNJABI RECIPE

Feliqus ™
Chicken & Rabbit Biryani
The no.1 petfood for Sikh cats
IN MANGO CHUTNEY
MADE TO TRADITIONAL PUNJABI RECIPE!

Feliqus ™
Lamb Of God
e no.1 petfood for Catholic cats
IN HOLY GRAVY
MADE BY THE ARCHANGEL ST. MICHAEL!

Feliqus ™
Matzah Ball Soup
no.1 petfood for Jewish cats
IN KUGEL JELLY
MADE TO TRADITIONAL KOSHER RECIPE!

CATS LIKE FELIQUS LIKE *Feliqus* ™
The no.1 pet food for religious cats

femash

Daily Mash
2011-2012

Women are being pressurised into emulating unrealistic levels of brainless folly, according to a new report

Celebrity culture making women feel insufficiently stupid

by **Jenny Houston**

RESEARCH by the Institute for Studies found that female celebrity role models like Katie Price, Paris Hilton and the triple-headed tit hydra that is the Kardashian sisters possessed a level of dim-wittedness which is unattainable for most women.

Professor Henry Brubaker said: "They're asking themselves questions like 'Am I stupid enough?', 'Can I ever fully exclude thoughts unrelated to sex and social status from my mind?' and 'Will I ever be just a dead-eyed, Ron-sealed-looking host organism for pretend boobs?'.

"Of course the answer is invariably 'no' and this is where neurosis begins."

He added: "We live in an age where everything wants to be stupid, but it's important to remember that there is more to life. Like, for example, being rich.

"Women must learn to be happy with their own personal stupidity - and perhaps set personal thickness goals, for example convincing themselves of one idiotic thing every day such as that kangaroos are a type of dog."

Teacher Emma Bradford said: "However hard I try and whatever products I use, I cannot make my brain the same as Khloe Kardashian's and that upsets me.

"It seems that however hard I try I am stuck with a level of intellect somewhat above the Heat magazine ideal.

"Sometimes, in a fit of self-loathing, I go and gorge myself on a book."

Mumsnet into some right filth

TERRIFYING online collective Mumsnet has revealed a predilection for high-grade filth.

The community website, which can bring down a rhino at 40 paces, has abandoned its support for online pornography filters after having a look at some of it.

Biting her bottom lip, a spokeswoman said: "Oh my. And they've only just met. Look at the size of his whatsit!

"Oh my."

Bookmarking a variety of things for later, she added: "Ultimately it is the parents' responsibility to ensure that children do not look at pornography by making sure that favourite sites are bookmarked with labels like 'car insurance' or 'Amnesty International'."

Since discovering online pornography the discussion threads on Mumsnet have veered from traditional subjects such as teething and clever things to do with carrots to sticky threesomes and clever things to do with carrots.

Meanwhile thousands of members have even logged in to Dadsnet in a bid to source the hottest mum-on-mum action live from Rotterdam.

How my husband's highly embarrassing penis complaint brought our street together

"I was making supper when my husband Lawrence arrived back from the doctor's, his face drained of colour"

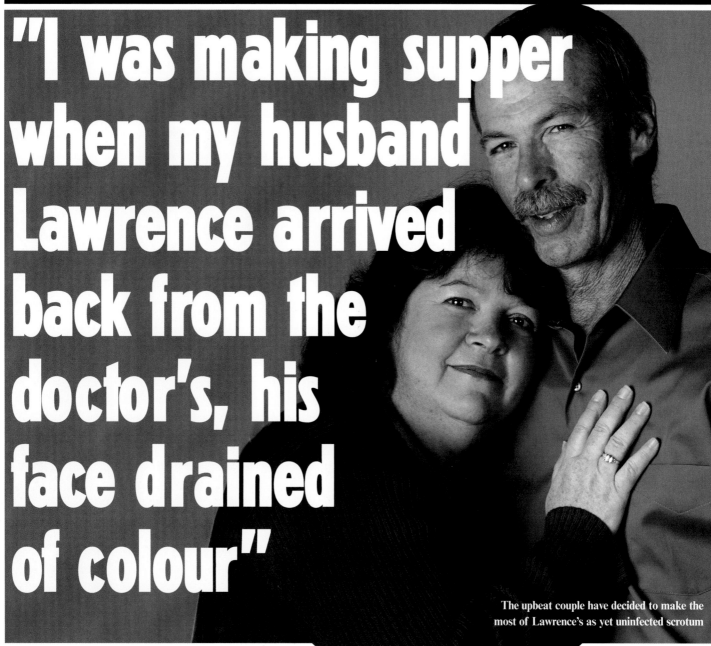

The upbeat couple have decided to make the most of Lawrence's as yet uninfected scrotum

"It's called Mobley's Syndrome," he said, "that's why my penis has shrunk to a fraction of its former size and acquired a pungent odour of stale limes. It's a rare bacterial thing. There are no other symptoms ... but there is no cure." I finished making supper, poured some wine and then held him.

by
Marjorie Hammil

MY HUSBAND is a private, discreet man, especially when it comes to matters of the penis. But I am a very determined woman, and even if his reproductive organ would never recover I was determined to prevent his condition from turning him into a recluse. While he was at work that day, I conceived the idea of a street party designed to both lift Lawrence's spirits and raise awareness of Mobley's Syndrome. As well as delicious food and great company, there would be talks and information about his condition. Brilliant!

Of course, it wasn't easy keeping the big event concealed from Lawrence.

Over the following weeks I was forced to make numerous excuses for my absence, for example saying that I had been attending a reptile husbandry seminar in Kent, when in fact I was next door, showing photos of Lawrence's shrivelling, malodorous foreskin to the neighbours.

Amazingly, the secret held until the big day. I'll never forget Lawrence's face as he rounded the corner to see 85 cheering people sit-

ting around a long picnic table beneath a banner reading WISHING YOU HAP-PENIS LAWRENCE. Initially he was so overwhelmed that he ran into the house, locking all the doors and windows. But he came out and had some cake the following day.

I have since written and sold two books about my husband's penis condition, one of which is to be made into a Hollywood film starring Tom Berenger. I have also made numerous television and radio appearances, and have recently begun a book about my 13-year-old nephew Tom, highlighting his addiction to masturbating onto crispbread.

Is the celebrity diet we recommended last week killing you?

The Institute for Studies' Professor Henry Brubaker analyses the daily diet of Frankie Sandford from The Saturdays to search for the potentially lethal carcinogens lurking within.

Breakfast

Frankie Sandford from the Saturdays says: I like Cheerios, 'cos they're like me, dead cheery and that. I have them with milk even though I'm scared of cows and milk's made of cow, isn't it? I wash it down with diet Sunny Delight as I am watching my figure.

Professor Brubaker says: Very few cows make it past the age of 15 and this is due to the large amount of milk in their diet from an early age. Cereal can be a healthy option but unfortunately many spoons contain many cancer-causing polishes.

Lunch

Frankie Sandford from the Saturdays says: If I'm doing a concert I can't have anything spicy 'cos it will mess up my voice for talking between the songs but generally speaking I like a juicy, hot piece of rump smothered in creamy sauce.

Professor Brubaker says: She may as well point a pistol full of Polonium bullets at her temple and pull the trigger.

Dinner

Frankie Sandford from the Saturdays says: Usually a light pasta salad, which is dead weird 'cos I didn't know you could make a pasta from a lettuce. When I was younger I liked Nandos but I can't have that any more 'cos it goes straight to my thighs, just like my dog.

Professor Brubaker says: Italy has more people battling cancer than any other country called Italy in the world so Frankie Sandford from The Saturdays may as well be sleeping in an X Ray machine.

If you have moods, personal issues, can't talk straight or make decisions and have a woman's sexual organs then you could very likely be a female boss.

Female bosses? YOU might as well torch the company

by **Amelia Raven**

A FASCINATING new study by Professor Julia Hanley from the University of Cincinnati has proved that female bosses do more to destroy business than recessions. It's taken years for female bosses to break through the glass ceiling, but the study shows they're destroying the companies they're working for in a similar manner to the way they devastate boxes of chocolate, white wine and men's egos.

Professor Hanley said: "Don't hire us, seriously, we're the equivalent of Dutch Elm disease for companies. You don't even know you've got the female boss fungus until you go into the accounts department and see it's withered remnants unable to send an email let alone balance a spreadsheet. We're the worst."

She added: "I'm bright, I'm efficient, I'm organised, but I'm also a woman and that means that at any moment I could cry, send all the staff home or have an episode in a board meeting where I start pulling someone's hair out because I'm jealous of something I'm not even aware of."

The study has also shown that ambitious women working to a female boss are ten times more likely to suffer from depression, anxiety and scabies than they are working for men.

Professor Hanley said: "If you're a woman and by some unfortunate cosmic twist of fate you end up working for a female you should quit immediately. Ever tried working for a human that's also a snake and a spider and drunk and automatically hates you? No, well, that's what it's like. It's called Queen 'I Will Destroy You With My Stinger Of Insecurity' Bee syndrome and it is unattractive.

"Women on women is a horrible combination in business, do us all a favour ladies and save it for the pornography."

Although there is evidence that women have increased profits in companies and regularly outperformed their male counterparts it later emerged the people collating the data were working for a woman and were therefore mentally unstable.

Professor Hanley added: "You try and tell a woman that she shouldn't be a boss because she's female and they take it so personally because they're so unbelievably fragile. The great thing about male bosses is that they're not competitive or self-centered and they're completely at ease around breasts."

Are you an annoying female boss?

Take this quiz to see if you're an annoying female boss:

1. Are you holding back productivity with your out of control emotions and capital sucking hormones?

2. When you first meet someone do you immediately think of ways you could mentally break them?

3. When you're in a meeting with a more attractive woman are you listening to what she's saying or just thinking about slapping the bitch in the face?

4. Have you built a bed into one of your desk drawers so you can always be in the office?

5. Do you sometimes defecate in the men's bathroom to show them they don't scare you?

6. Do you sing a song about your own success in the shower?

7. Do you think being duplicitous and cunning is cool?

8. When you're not thinking about work are you really still thinking about poisoning people's coffee?

9. Do you think women can be as good bosses as men?

10. Have you ever had a colleague followed just to fuck with them?

If you've answered yes to any of these questions you're a woman who is at work in a boss position. Shame on you. And you're probably a terrible mother as well.

NANNÉX PARIS

We road test the latest beauty products that will have jealous, spiteful women across the country drooling over how brave you are.

Hot Heartbreak Make Up

WHETHER your MP husband has been found in a dungeon with half a pound of Dundee cake up his back passage or your footballer boyfriend has admitted why he's been on antibiotics since his team's tour of Asia, your make up needs to stand up to the pap walk to the local shops.

Clinix Waterproof Mascara: £30

Clinix scientists tested this by forcing a glamour model to chop onions while they read out the texts on her boyfriend's mobile and cut up her platinum credit cards. She then had to do a four-hour appearance in a Magaluf nightclub dodging sexual assaults in 90 degree heat. Result – not a single smear! Recommended.

Bijon Combined Foundation/Concealer: £28

It's 7am and you've been awake all night as your private investigator lists all the brothels your backbench MP husband has been visiting over the last six months. The press have been tipped off and are swarming outside the gates of your home. You've managed to sob every drop of water from your body and your face is blotchier than a dalmation's scrotum but you still need to pop to the shops with your kids to show everyone you're still a strong family unit. Bijon's little pot of miracles will be the difference between being described as 'Drawn but dignified' and 'who could blame him?'. Essential.

Perlist Eyeshadow: £14

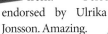

A bag of frozen peas and a shopping trip to Harvey Nichols by way of apology is all very well, but a telephoto lens can pick up a black eye from half a mile away. Perlist's patented DVGO technology will make you look Hollywood-starlet-fresh! Personally endorsed by Ulrika Jonsson. Amazing.

HAVE you ever felt like your man loves his car more than he loves you? With clean, sleek lines free of sagging and varicose veins, it's small wonder your husband would rather run a chamois along its shining bonnet than your mottled, orange-peel thighs.

Fortunately though help is at hand from Devina Hartley-Kalden's Auto-Erotic Body Modification Boutique. She said: "We make women feel sexy again by replacing parts of their bodies with automobile components.

The result is that their husbands love to polish them in a doting manner, and are less likely to fuck other women."

Here's a few highlights from her range:

by
Suzy McKenzie

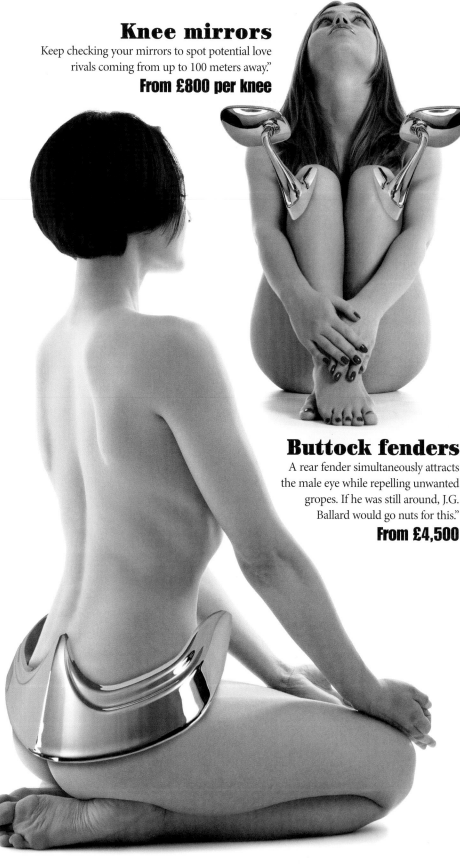

Knee mirrors

Keep checking your mirrors to spot potential love rivals coming from up to 100 meters away."
From £800 per knee

Buttock fenders

A rear fender simultaneously attracts the male eye while repelling unwanted gropes. If he was still around, J.G. Ballard would go nuts for this."
From £4,500

Are YOU

Back ornaments
Have a stag, a golfer or a kestrel welded onto your spine. Elegantly cast in pewter, these are perfect for husbands wanting to personalise their wives."
From £40-£850

Breastlights
Eye-catching halogen breast substitutes, with switches allowing you to dip the beams when seated in someone's line of sight."
From £1,500 - £3,400

Armwheels
Bedroom-wise these are perfect for when you're in the wheelbarrow position but want that extra mobility. Also, carrying the additional weight of these stylish hand replacements tones and sculpts your arms.
From £900 per arm

auto-erotic?

2,500 Domestic Animals. 2 Judges. 1 Competition.

masterChef
The Pets

INCREDIBLE COOKERY LIKE YOU'VE NEVER SEEN:

Starts Monday 42nd July only on BBC one

"Mr. Tibley! You're eating the ingredients for your Sauce Vierge again!"

"That better not be one of your own legs in that rabbit casserole!"

Health tips to prevent you having to go and see that Bangladeshi chap who's probably not even a real vet

by Margaret Gerving

'My evening stool is at least an hour early'

'It'll have you running like a clockwork pig'

Staying regular

Dear Margaret,

Ever since I can remember, I've made stool at 8am and 8pm, regular as you like. In fact my husband used to call me his little pooclock. But I've noticed recently that my evening motions are banging on the door by 7pm. Should I be worried?

Yours,

Elizabeth Wilson

Dear Elizabeth,

I'm sure there's absolutely no cause for alarm but our Edith on my mother's side started needing an extra evacuation in the early afternoon and three weeks later they were putting her in the ground. The doctors said it was her heart that gave out but he hardly knew a word of English so I take that with a pinch of salt. I've always sworn by sago pudding to slow everything down, try that.

Vomit

Dear Margaret,

I keep vomiting blood and I've lost three stone in a fortnight. Also there is some blood leaking from my left eye.

I'm sorry for writing to you, I hate to cause a fuss.

Yours,

Emma Bradford

Dear Emma,

Somebody loves to be centre of attention, don't they?

A bit of hard work will get you back on your feet, young lady.

For a start, I bet your nets wouldn't suffer for a boil wash.

'This trollop is fooling nobody'

Skin

Dear Margaret,

What's this? Is it a mole or a freckle or what? (drawing enclosed).

Yours,

Alice Jamieson

Dear Alice,

If you heat up a darning needle and give it a jab it should clear up in no time. They're just nature's way of getting rid of your bad thoughts so you've no need to hang on to it.

Our Arthur was covered in them but when you look at what he married it's no wonder. Give it a swab with Sarson's after to keep it clean.

HYPNOTIC WARDROBE

This wardrobe is so compelling... yet it's impossible to say why.

"I... can't ... stop ... looking ..."
Nikki Hollis, Exeter

"Must...obey...wardrobe..."
Tom Logan, Surrey

You will buy the wardrobe. It is inevitable.

The price of the wardrobe is irrelevant.

You don't find the wardrobe, the wardrobe will find you.

Guardian sports supplement still number one choice for lighting middle-class barbecues

'I see the Wolverhampton Wanderers have made a good start to the league'

THE Guardian's Weekend Sport supplement has retained its title as the number one choice for lighting middle class barbecues.

According to figures from the Institute for Studies, the perennially-unread pull-out section was ignited 18,051 times during the last 12 weeks, in order that organic lamb cutlets and Waitrose Halloumi and Pepper Skewers might be satisfactorily undercooked.

Guardian reader Stephen Malley said: "I don't want to burn the main paper, obviously. Or the Guide, from which I have gleaned sufficient knowledge of dubstep to still wear trainers.

"The magazine has an interview with Miranda Hart that Susie wanted to read, the Work and Family bits are usually very important and the Money section has something about fixed-rate ISAs.

"So by a process of elimination, we have a winner. Although if there's a black athlete on the cover I might remove that first because I'm not a racist."

During the winter months Malley uses the supplement for wrapping a brie, covering the table so Olivia and Jake can do finger-painting and putting wellies on after a nice walk along the beach at Southwold.

Guardian Sports correspondent Roy Hobbs said: "We haven't updated the contents of 'The Firestarter' for nine years now.

"As long as we stick a different cricketer on the front now and again, no one actually notices. We could print a nude photo of Megan Fox holding up the meaning of life on page five and no-one would be any the wiser.

"Still, at least it's not the motoring section in The Observer."

Royal buttocks

Whether smiling at us from carriages or declaring things open, Britain's royal family is never less than godlike. And ever since the first cave dweller was anointed with an iron age crown made of bronze, they have been equipped with serenely regal bottoms. We take a look at some of the most famous sovereign bottoms since the dawn of time...

Boudica

Historians think that the modern term 'booty', denoting a lady's nether region, originated from Boudica's name which in the Iceni language literally meant "Lovely handful". The warrior queen headed an army of 10,000 fiercely-loyal fighters who would follow her into skirmishes just to get a glimpse of her cheeks jiggling in her chariot. After unprecedented victories against the occupying Roman army earned her the Latin nickname Rectum Supremus, she was ultimately defeated in the battle of Watling Street when a traitorous Celtic general spiked her battlecacks with hemlock.

Eleanor Of Aquitaine

The medieval queen instigated the second Holy Crusade to recapture the pants worn by the Virgin Mary, said to be held in the Sacred Linen Cupboard of Jerusalem. Hundreds of knights died to return the holiest of unmentionables back into Christian hands, which were believed to bestow eternally pert buttocks to those who wore them. Extrovert for a woman of her era, a tapestry in the Palace of Poitiers depicts Eleanor parading through the court with the top band of the Holy G String showing above her bustle.

through the ages

Queen Victoria

The monarch banned buttocks during her 63-year reign, as she felt they risked reminding men of bosoms. Despite her era being one of unprecedented achievements in the fields of science, industry and taking countries from brown people who didn't know what to do with them, it notably lacks a single winner of the ancient title 'Rear Of The Year'. Despite this, she managed to produce nine children, although old palace equipment shows that if Prince Albert wanted to get the engines started he was only allowed to squeeze her unamused seat of power through a complex series of steam-powered ropes and pulleys attached to an articulated brass hand.

Pippa Middleton
Dirty. Little. Bitch.

Queen Elizabeth I

Britain's greatest monarch famously died without any of the many crown princes of Europe getting their hands on her Tudor tush. The allure of her unsullied poopsie reached almost mythical proportions in her lifetime, culminating in her address to the troops at Tilbury docks, in which she said: "I know I have the body of a weak and feeble woman but I have the heart and stomach of a king, not to mention buns you could bounce a goat off." A notoriously vain woman, she still insisted on having her behind complimented right up until the end of her reign, despite contemporary reports likening it to "Two sackes of oats after a ferret hath been at them".

Looters return stuff to Games Workshop

SCORES of disappointed rioters queued up this morning to return goods they had mistakenly looted from Games Workshop.

What the bloody hell are these when they're at home?

The crestfallen thieves had raided the store hoping for a PS3 or Nintendo bounty but arrived home to find they had stolen a box containing 300 unpainted Orcs and a board game called Beyond the Ultraforest of Kwang.

Martin Bishop, 19, said: "I am returning The Runering of Fangor.

"It includes two dice, each with about 40 sides and instructions on how to gain the trust of a 'cloud wizard'.

"And yet somehow I'm the fucking bad guy."

He added: "Nevertheless I am now immune to Dwarven magic, so it hasn't been a complete waste of time."

Meanwhile, historical kitsch outlet Past Times reported the return of a pair or resin bookends in the shape of the Egyptian cat-god Sekhmet and 254 teak statues of a fat, reclining Buddha.

And in Manchester, people who stole copies of Limitless starring Bradley Cooper have been setting fire to them and throwing them back through the window of HMV.

Roy Hobbs, manager of Games Workshop in Birmingham, said: "Welcome home my children. Let me bathe you in the healing milk of Fagnarbarak.

"I knew we would meet again."

Daily Mash

WeekeND

2011-2012

Professor
Brian Cox

Why outer
space wants
you DEAD

ANDY MURRAY
A Day in the Life

FOOD STYLE
Are you wearing beef gloves?

DR MORRIS O'CONNOR
Self Help? Help Yourself!

TV guide, Film reviews

PLUS:
Some pills that might make
you feel normal for a change

The Ken Bruce Easy Recliner

After a long, hard day, what better way to unwind than relaxing in the comforting sound of Ken Bruce reading out a letter about cabbages?

The Ken Bruce Easy Recliner features twelve speakers positioned at the shoulders, knees and ankles to provide deep penetration of soft Scottish burr into joints and muscles, gently massaging you into a state of contented stupor.

With six separate settings from "Light banter" to "Jaunty flirtation", the worries of the day will melt away as Ken's mellifluous jocularity soaks deep into the pores to provide a mild euphoria without the need for prescription painkillers or vodka.

Research has proven* that inoffensive chitchat can tackle a number of medical complaints from rheumatoid arthritis to piles as the rich, rounded vowels of Ken Bruce are pumped directly into the body.

All for just £899

*Research results still pending from the European Institute For Disc Jockey Complimentary Medicine

BBCFURNITURE

Your Frankie Sandford from The Saturdays, Saturday catch-up

This week Frankie has...

Borrowed a library book on tropical fish

Returned a faulty kettle to Dixons

Accompanied the Carlisle historical society on a dig of some Roman baths

Failed an NVQ in social care

Built a complicated Airfix spitfire

Pretended to fancy a tramp

Brian Cox's Terrors of the Cosmos

Hi, I am Brian Cox, the keyboard player in 90s dance-pop faves D:Ream. When not doing my proper job of playing uplifting, anthemic house music in nightclubs, I enjoy my hobby of science, a subject about which I have amassed many books. All types of science are interesting but my best is space. Space is massive, it's bigger than the biggest car. Unfortunately, it is also very dangerous. Not only is going there an insult to God, you'll probably die. I hope that if you ever get the chance to go there, you stay in and watch telly instead.

Bum Holes

Normally bums are funny, but not these ones. They can suck you in from over a metre away, then spit you back out as an 'energy turd'.

Alsatians and monkeys

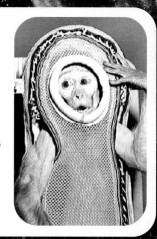

In the sixties we sent a lot of alsatians and monkeys into space to see how far they could get before they exploded. But some of them crashed into planets and survived. On some planets the alsatians and the monkeys teamed up. This is the case on Mars. If you land there the dogs will bite your genitals while the monkeys bite your face. It's a special attack they've worked out between them.

Massive meteor with fists

Meteors are so tough. Millions of years ago one landed on Earth and beat up all the dinosaurs before flying off again.

Bits of old space ships

If a spaceship breaks or the astronauts get bored of it, they just leave it in space. Floating around. Ready to crash into you and explode.

Frozen human waste

When astronauts' toilets fill up, it all gets fired out in a big block of ice, same as a plane. Loads of frozen astronaut pee with your name on it.

Space seaweed

Space is often described as being like an ocean. The famous science fiction writer Arthur C Clarke once wrote that 'the universe is like a sea with all stuff floating in it'. What do seas have? Seaweed. Except space seaweed is full of acid that will burn your hands off.

Aliens from the film Alien

These aliens will jump down your throat and then explode from your stomach, like a service station sandwich.

Predator

Because of his heat-proof armour, Predator can live on the sun. He has a house made of human spines, and is planning an extension.

Space

Heaven

THE
BRITISH
MUSEUM

THE STUFF OF TUTANKHAMUN EXHIBITION

Greatest of all the pharaohs, Tutankhamun had a shit ton of stuff.

Now we've got a big heap of it at the British Museum: gold stuff, jewelled stuff, a cool mummified cat and this other thing that looks like a beetle

Why not come and have a look? It's a good way to kill an afternoon

THE STUFF OF TUTANKHAMUN EXHIBITION
British Museum
London
Admission: Guilt-based donation
Mon-Fri: 10ish-whenever
Sat: Afternoons
Sun: Unlikely

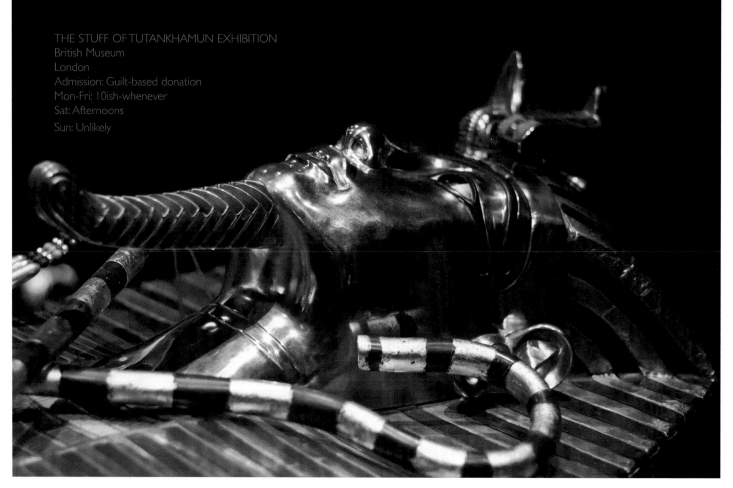

Stephen Gately
in Hell

TO BE honest, you kind of get into a routine with the tortures after a while. We're on a daily rotation between the lake of fire, the crater of suffering and the chalet of genital electrification. But despite this small consolation of mundanity, if I had my time again I definitely would've done things differently.

One of the funny things about Hell, or 'The Hot Place' as I prefer to call it, is that it looks exactly like the pictures in our old school bible. Something about the way it's lit even gives it a woodcut-esque quality. Certainly the supposedly old-fashioned conception of damnation is pretty much right on the money. Had I known that when I was on a podium at Trade, dancing to hard house with a bottle of amyl up my nose and a footballer hanging out of my leather trousers I would've ... well ... left immediately, gone home and put on some sensible slacks and relentlessly read Bernard Cornwell books until I was heterosexual.

The Hot Place is divided into a number of suburbs, or 'circles', of increasing grimness. The circle you end up in depends on how gay you were. I'm in the fifth circle because I was a pretty bad gay, but not as bad as, for example, Freddy Mercury, who was properly into Thai renters and whatnot. Freddy is in the innermost circle. I don't even want to talk about that, it's really yucky. The outer or first circle is reserved for less bad gays, who didn't really force it down people's throats (figuratively speaking) like some of us. Gays who were only dirty in amusing, subtle ways like Frankie Howerd and the one from Are You Being Served? It's where Christopher Biggins will end up.

Obviously I hate myself a lot for being gay and for ending up here. Sometimes, when I'm being lowered into the lake of fire by a cackling goblin, I try to think about good, non-gay things as a form of self-improvement. Things like home-made preserves, heterosexual family life and the brave soldiers fighting to protect our nation. But then I start thinking about the soldiers' khaki pants and bulging muscles and I start fancying them. Gaah! It's almost like I was meant to be gay. But of course I know now that homosexuality is not natural, so obviously I wasn't.

The other thing I think about a lot is Heaven. My bum is really sore from being poked with tridents and I would just love to rest it on a lovely soft cloud, in a calm peaceful environment with harps or Brian Eno's ambient albums playing in the background. I bet Heaven is really nice and tasteful. But not, of course, in a gay way.

'I bet Heaven is really nice and tasteful. But not, of course, in a gay way'

A Day In The Life Of...

Andy Murray

7.30am:
Wake up. I've been waking up since I was a kid growing up in Scotland and I keep focussing on getting better and better at it. Bit disappointed with today's effort as I immediately fell back asleep for a couple of hours. Apparently Rafael Nadal sleeps standing up in his bed, already dressed.

9.30am:
Breakfast of cereal, orange juice and painkillers to numb the soreness in my cruciate caused by stretching to get the bowl down from the cupboard. I remember being in the breakfast bar during an ATP event and seeing Federer handing out cutlery to everyone in the hotel for two hours solid without missing a beat.

11.00am:
Light training in the gym working on building my upper body strength on the advice of my coach – I regret firing him now as my carpal tunnel flared up writing out his sacking email.

Arrive to find Djokovic on the running machine, which is showing 27 miles. He holds a ten-minute conversation with me in perfect English until I need a sit-down from carrying my heavy kit bag. He carries on running and I can't help notice his shirt is dry as a bone.

2.00pm:
Practice session with the serving machine. It beats me in straight sets, 6-3, 6-2, 6-3. I think my mobility about the court was better than the 300kg automaton but his groundstrokes were just a different class.

5.00pm:
Charity dinner at Wimbledon. All the greats of the game are there. When I arrive and the maître d' shows me to my table, I think about asking him why I'm sat in the corridor but by the time I work out what to say, he's already off to get Soderling some more champagne flutes. I toy with the plastic flower on my table for a while until I accidentally dislocate two knuckles.

8.00pm:
Early night. Before retiring to bed I check the ATP rankings on their website to see if I'm still 4th best in the world at tennis. I am. I mouth the word 'third' to myself and touch the framed Jeremy Bates photo above my PC, which falls off the wall and breaks a toe. I limp to bed to get some rest and as I switch off the light, across the road Jo-Wilfried Tsonga's house party gets underway and I'm kept awake until 4am by his stereo blasting out Johnny Halliday records. I'd move house if I could afford it.

In today's fast-paced, competitive world it's no longer enough for your food to simply taste delicious – it has to be fashionably dressed

Food stylist DEBBY KENYON takes you through this season's hot food looks

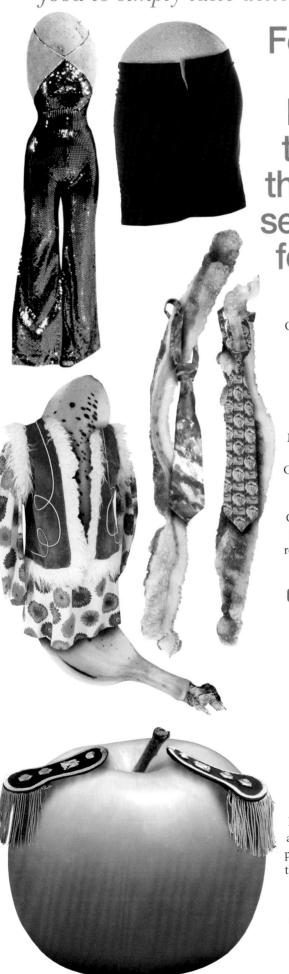

BACON CRAVATS

Give your bacon a dangerous, rakish charm with these cad-esque cravats. Bacon should wear neck garments with a loose single knot.

APPLE-LETS

Military-style epaulets lend a touch of 'Officer and a Gentleman' to your fruit bowl.

BEEF GLOVES

Gloves aren't just for winter – they can look stylish all year round, especially when they're on beef.

ORANGE PENCIL SKIRTS

Sexy, simple citrus chic.

POTATO PLAYSUITS

There's nothing like a sassy one-piece retro playsuit to bring out the innate cheekiness of the potato. It's like something out of Charlie's Angel's, if Farah Fawcett were a Maris Piper.

ETHNIC BANANA WAISTCOATS

Hippy chic is big this season, and these batik waistcoats are perfect for giving your banana the laid-back Woodstock vibe.

CURRY FASCINATORS

Accessorise your lamb bhuna with a vintage fascinator for instant Great Gatsby-esque glamour.

'Self-help' is something we can all do. The expression 'self-help' comes from the English phrase 'help yourself' which is often used for getting guests, who have stayed over for the night, to make their own breakfast.

Being the doorman to the nightclub in your brain

Power Thinking with DR MORRIS O'CONNOR

I WAS adverse to self-help for many years believing it to be the pastime of fools, losers, dicks, knobs, knob heads and people in catering. I said to my then girlfriend, "Lindsay, I'm already better than 75%, nay, 80% of the people I know, why would I want to get better? If you think you can do better, by all means try, but you're a seven at best and with only four GCSEs and that droopy eye what level businessman do you realistically think you're going to get? Maybe, someone in low level ad sales, maybe." "Morris, I've got an idea for a revenue generating website, you better start acting right towards me," she replied. We did eventually break up and she went on to marry a butcher with large hands.

The conversation stuck and I realised I had something to learn, there was room for improvement. I wanted to help myself, but how? I certainly wasn't going to listen to anyone, I was better than that.

After we broke up I spent a lot of time imaging what Lindsey was up to with the butcher and not in a good way. Positions, conversations, them laughing about me on a cycling holiday in Wales, him analysing her eczema? I told her it was just dried skin behind her ears, but she wouldn't listen.

Thoughts of them haunted my dreams like a ghost of them had they both died in a boating accident and then got into my brain and specifically into the dream section. It was taunting me in the day too and after a week I realised every thought I thunk or thoughted was doing me no favours. Did I always think like this? I couldn't remember. I had kept a Thought Diary since I was 17, a diary of thoughts that I detailed with a thought recorder or biro. I quickly sought it out and flicking through the pages frantically, I came to May 14th 1997...

Location: IBM Portsmouth canteen
Time: 12.48
Hair: Gel and spray
Sweat level: Medium to light spotting

Thoughts: I think I like LL Cool J. Gummy Bears! Bouncing here and there and everywhere! I miss those guys. (4 x minutes thinking about Gummy Bears). Could I create a new type of nut, Morris Nuts? A trans-crumble oil nut. A high oil-yielding nut that's also good for crumbling, a nut that you could crumble on anything, even things outside of the food world. Oh look there's the receptionist from floor three, I would love to see her boobs unleashed and jiggling in a strong coastal wind.

Good classic thoughts, nothing wrong with them, but suddenly it hit me, none of these thoughts were that cool or earning me any money. If I was to improve, to help myself, I had to do it in my brain. I had to control it and run it like a fancy west London nightclub and only let the attractive, well-dressed and rich thoughts in. I had to create 'Luka' the door guy and become a bitchy, sharp talking door whore, insulting everyday thoughts and if necessary getting Vinny my brain's nightclub bouncer to rough them up a bit.

Night after night everyday thoughts tried to get into my brain. 'Sorry you're not on the list,' Luka would say not even looking at them. 'But we're fun thoughts about getting a dog, please can we come into the nightclub?' they would plead. 'Yeah and who's that at the back?' 'That's a thought about the butcher and Lindsay doing it on a weights bench in a gymnasium.' 'Vinny! Vinny! We gotta big problem on the door!' It got messy, regular thoughts were finding their way in, posing as staff. One time Luka discovered two physically short thoughts about Party Poppers trying to get in by doing a shoulder ride inside a long Mackintosh.

After a month of trying the rubbish thoughts got the message and my brain became so exclusive it was even courting celebrity thoughts. In May 2008 one of Madonna's thoughts about affordable black support tights for her dancers in the Sweet and Sticky Tour was in my brain for over an hour.

With a strict thought policy my brain is now ten times as efficient, churning out streams of business ideas and ways of shortening my work commute. The only time Lindsay and the butcher can get to me is when I see them in real life, like when he hand fed her spring rolls at the opening of the new Chinese in town or when they openly snogged right next to me in the start queue of the Portsmouth half marathon. Am I thinking about it after the fact? Not with Luka and Vinny around.

Gardening with STEPHEN MALLEY

Biodegradable bags

IF ANYTHING has ever given me more pleasure than a nice hibiscus on a balmy late summer afternoon, it's watching my wife's face turn beet-red as I choked the life out of her evil fucking body. The deed done, I sit here in the living room of our cottage, hands stinking of death as her body cools in the bath.

As I sit here, gazing out over the verandah as a finger of evening sun slips from between the clouds to illuminate my favourite rhododendron bush, I ponder the next step. It's not as if the bitch's body is going to bury itself. But the

stiffening remains are heavy and cumbersome, besides being person-shaped even when bagged and thus a beacon for beady-eyed neighbours.

A doctor and his wife live next door. They're originally from Manchester and right nosey fuckers. I wonder briefly if I should kill them too, but it seems excessive. Earlier I tried to cut her foot off but it was surprisingly resilient, like a well-established tree root. I hardly broke the skin. But then, those shears have never been very good, even when sharpened regularly. The chainsaw. That's what I'll do. The chainsaw. Put down newspaper, remove

all her clothes, probably strip off myself because of all the flying viscera, and get about her with the chainsaw. Bag the bits in those Waitrose carriers she always insisted on saving, sling them on the compost heap then conceal with a generous layer of mulch. Hose down the gore-coated bathroom walls, stick her clothes in the wood burner, call the police saying I'm worried because it's eight hours since she went to the bottle bank, open a decent claret and congratulate myself on a job well done.

Also this month, don't forget to sprinkle potash on your pansies.

Charlie Reeves' Movie Review

I Melt With You (15)

An ambitious outing from Mothman Prophecies director Mark Pellington whose fourth film had purported to be a dark thrilling character study, set during a 'Big Chill' festival scenario. And with Rob Lowe (Perfect Strangers) heading up a cast of 40-something recreational drug users, the film certainly promised to be the choice offering at this year's Sundance Film festival which I was happy to attend.

Unfortunately I got on the wrong plane and instead of ending up in Utah I ended up in Qatar, where the film was not being shown.

The Adventures of Tin Tin (12)

When I first learnt that my boyhood hero would be rendered into a movie franchise I was like many, excited. And with master story teller Steven Spielberg at the helm, along with a cast including Simon Pegg (Hot Fuzz) and Andy Serkis (Gollum) I was certain this would be a thrilling rollercoaster treasure hunt that would have me on the edge of my seat. Unfortunately I was not warned about the strobe lighting in an early sea-storm scene, which triggered my Occipital Lobe Epilepsy resulting in me having a grand mal seizure. I came round on a cinema carpet, spitting blood and teeth and sadly saw little of this film.

Happy Feet 2 (PG)

This second anthropomorphic bird outing sees Mumble the penguin in a fatherly role, attempting to teach his own son the importance of expression through dance. Although sequels are rarely better than the originals, I went into this one with an open mind.

I also went in with hooping cough which resulted in someone's fat dad demanding I leave the cinema instantly. When I got up to oblige someone threw an unopened can of Lilt at me and I fell backwards off the balcony. I think it's about penguins.

BBC1	BBC2	ITV1	CHANNEL 4	CHANNEL 5
4.30 Gimme a Break People write in to Sir Jimmy Saville and he goes to their house and breaks their jaw.	**4.30 The Hairy Bikers' Food Tour of Britain** Not as nice as they seem.	**4.30 Midsomer Murders** Once again we ask: Why bother making any other television programmes?	**4.30 Buggery or No Buggery** Game show about anal intercourse.	**4.30 Big Brother** Kill yourself.
5.15 Horrible Histories The BBC's ongoing effort to condition our youth to believe the British Empire was worse than Pol Pot.	**5.30 Flog It!** Harder and harder until you learn your lesson.	**5.30 The Chase** No idea, but it sounds marvellously exciting.	**5.00 Buggery Trip** A rickety coach full of sodomites.	**5.00 Crime Scene: Navy Crime** Someone steals a submarine, but then brings it back.
5.45 Newsround See above.	**6.00 Ten of the Best** Extra-strength condoms, no doubt.	**6.00 Regional News** A thing about a lovely charity who did a thing.	**5.30 Come Buggery with Me** Get some people round your house and then enter them.	**5.30 Big Brother** Why haven't you killed yourself?
6.00 News at Six Twenty-five-minutes about Africa while your gas bill goes through the roof.	**6.30 Put Your Money Where Your Mouth Is** And your mouth where your toilet is.	**6.30 ITV News and Weather** News from your perspective. For a change!	**6.00 The Simpsons** Homer sodomises a minor character voiced by Gary Glitter.	**6.00 Crime Scene: Navy Crime** Jethro falls off an old bicycle.
6.30 Regional news Government cutback sob stories in your area.	**7.00 Eggheads** Horribly misleading.	**7.00 Emmerdale** Archie has a secret about Gemma. It's okay, it's a nice secret.	**6.30 Buggeryoaks** Samantha catches Geoff and Andy doing buggery for the 40th week in a row.	**6.30 Big Brother** Have you got a car and a hosepipe?
7.00 The One Show Acceptable family entertainment though often treads the fine line between japery and criminal filth.	**7.30 Dragons' Den** Sell half your widget to a creepy Scotsman.	**7.30 Grimefighters** Filth removal. Magnificent.	**7.00 Channel Buggery News** Who's up who.	**7.00 Crime Scene: Navy Crime** A yacht is attacked with a crossbow.
8.00 EastEnders Kat wants Alfie to puke up in her face during sex. Probably.	**8.30 The Great British Bake Off** Cakes shaped like vulvas and a chocolate eclair with cream squirting out one end.	**8.30 Cops with Cameras** But not guns, unfortunately.	**7.55 The Political Slot** Being filled by a left-wing penis.	**8.00 Big Brother** What about a plastic bag and some string?
8.30 Holby City Expect a severely beaten gay.	**9.00 The Boy in the Striped Pyjamas** [Film] **(2008)** The Daily Mash did not support Herr Hitler's regime. Not at first anyway.	**10.00 ITV News at Ten and Weather** Pay attention. These are the Important Things.	**8.00 International Athletics: 4x400m buggery finals** It's not even nine o'clock.	**8.30 Crime Scene: Navy Crime** The sexual tension escalates.
9.00 Harry's Arctic Heroes His Royal Highness shows his playful side. Watch while standing up.	**10.30 Newsnight** Fucking nonsense.	**10.30 Dreamcatcher** [Film] **(2003)** Wesley Branson stars as a 1950s baseball player who wins the Kentucky Derby on a goat. Clean.	**9.30 Inside Nature's Buggering Giants** Scientists peer up something's rectum with a torch.	**9.00 Big Brother** Go on, jump off a bridge.
10.00 BBC News Goebbels with fancy music.	**11.15 India on Four Wheels** And £500m worth of licence payers' money	**Go to bed**	**10.30 Shameless** Unmissable fly-on-the-wall documentary about a Liverpool housing estate where no-one has worked since Napoleon.	**9.30 Crime Scene: Navy Crime** The sexual tension dissipates.
10.30 Donor Mum: The Children I've Never Met Eye-popping filth.	**11.50 The Tudors** Magnificent costumes and historically inaccurate intercourse.		**11.30 Chris Moyles' Buggery Night** Fat man asks famous people questions about sodomy.	**10.00 Big Brother** You'll get it over the back of your throat if you mix it with Drambuie.
11.30 Is Breast Best? Yes, and so is not having a job, you feminist whores.	**Go to bed**		**Got to bed**	**10.30 Crime Scene: Navy Crime** Wise-cracking man gets comeuppance. At sea.
Got to bed				**11.00 Big Brother** We're doing this again tomorrow.
				Go to bed.

The Simpsons
Channel 4, 6.00pm
Gary Glitter stars

Money Mash

THE DAILY MASH   2011 - 2012

Clever men
say good thing
bad thing now

Bad money thing make new scary time

Bad money thing make world have big new scary time, clever men say now.

NOISY room where shirty men swap zeroes have frowny day as lazy bones in sunny places say no money now and be sad.

And wide place with shouty fat people also have no money and all say nice brown man in big house is rubbish now.

Clever men say new scary time not that new, just new bit of spend-money-no-have big-scary-bad-thing.

But very big scary thing is clever men say not know how to make nice happy money time.

Fancy clever man with big proper job say: "Not know. Oh dear. Not know. You know? Tell please."

He say only six people have happy money time now and you and me be poor stinkies who live in dirty box near choo-choo house.

Fancy clever man then go back to bed and pull blanket over frowny face.

But stupid nobody man who no have fancy proper job say all must make good shiny thing.

He say: "Swap shiny thing for happy money to buy more good shiny thing.

"All happy smile when every place make good shiny thing. Even shouty fats and lazy bones.

"Then every day be happy money swap time. Hurray! Hurray!

"Right now fucked though."

Middle classes take lessons in looting

THOUSANDS of middle class people worried about job security have signed up for a two week course in looting.

With the economy plunging once more into the abyss, middle income professionals keen to maintain their standard of living are now learning how to smash a really big window, grab a Dualit toaster and run like fuck.

Stephen Malley, senior retail analyst at Donnelly-McPartlin, said: "Britain needs to loot its way out of recession. We could continue to dick about with spending cuts and taxation, but why bother when we can all just go apeshit in a John Lewis?"

Meanwhile, after a record breaking weekend of liberating small and medium-sized electronic goods across north London, the capital's leading looters have found their expertise in high demand.

Martin Bishop, a 19 year-old who specialises in microwaves, said: "I'm starting classes next week in a burned out Currys.

"For the first lesson we'll just be handling breeze blocks, passing them round the class, so everyone can get a feel for them.

"The following week everyone will get their own practice window to smash and then I'll show them how to get inside the shop without gouging themselves in the groin."

He added: "It's all about quick decisions. This isn't Currys on a Saturday afternoon, this is Currys at one o'clock on a Sunday morning with 15 rozzers outside, all of whom are tremendously keen to fuck you up.

"You have to go in there having memorised exactly what you want. Also - and this is something that middle class women always forget - you have to be able to carry it."

But Jane Thompson, a landscape architect from Finsbury Park, said she was forming a local co-operative so that busy working mothers can get together early in the morning to have coffee and loot very large appliances.

She added: "We'll take it in turns to choose something hefty. I'd like a Smeg fridge, but some weeks it might be a dishwasher or a piano.

"Why should a global depression stop my children from learning the piano when there's a perfectly nice one just sitting there?

"Would you like to see my sledge hammer? It's Javanese."

Credit card debtors sleeping like babies

MOST people are managing a sumptuous eight hours sleep a night despite crippling credit card debt, it has emerged.

Researchers have exploded the myth that people with large debts lie awake worrying about bailiffs after finding that most snuggle happily under an Egyptian cotton duvet cover they will never actually pay for.

Professor Henry Brubaker, of the Institute for Studies, said: "Increasingly people are recognising that there's no heaven and even if there was, St Peter would probably tell the bailiffs to go piss up a rope.

"What are they going to do? Jump in your coffin and wait there until you set up a direct debit?

"So we basically have two choices. Stop buying stuff - it's all shit anyway. Or buy an insane amount of stuff, sign up with one of those unusual companies that somehow negotiates half of it into oblivion and then eventually die.

"The credit card people will get all upset but it serves them right for

She's counting iPods jumping over smoothie makers

doing something so boring in the first place."

Helen Archer, a receptionist from Stevenage, said: "I may have £16,000 of credit card debt that's going nowhere fast, but the entire country is up to its nipples in someone else's money.

"Asking me if I can sleep at night, is like asking a leper living in a leper colony if he worries about facial lesions.

"If I see a sleep deprived David Cameron, unable to make eye contact with anyone, standing outside Number 10 announcing he has to send 88% of the country into prison for not paying its bills, I might make some hot chocolate."

She added: "I'll tell you what does keep me awake at night – the thought of having to live in a bio-sphere.

"I don't know why, I just think it would be shit."

Boost to recovery as everything becomes much more expensive

BRITAIN was well on the road to economic recovery today after the government made everything less affordable.

With unemployment at its highest since the discovery of machines in 1462, ministers said the best way to tackle it was to make sure no-one could buy things from shops.

Chancellor George Osborne said: "Deficit, Britain, responsibility, angry Chinamen, live within our means, Britain, economics of the madhouse, boom and bust my arse and if you think I'm paying that for an iPod you must be out of your fucking mind."

Meanwhile the boss of Britain's biggest food retailer stressed it was absolutely right that the government had made everything more expensive apart from food.

Tesco chief executive, Sir Terry Leahy, said: "Why would you want to buy a new telly when you can spend hours staring at this gorgeous packet of honey roast ham?

"You could even buy two and then prop them up against each other so that they form a little tent and then make some cowboys from bits of VAT-free cheddar. It's Brokeback Mountain in 3D but without the need for cumbersome spectacles."

Tom Logan, a former consumer from Peterborough, said: "I don't know much about economics, then again neither did John Maynard Keynes but everyone still listened to him for about a thousand years before realising he was full of hot piss.

"So anyway, my theory is, instead of taking more of my money and making things more expensive, let me keep my money so I can spend it in shops and the people who work in the shops can keep getting paid because I've bought stuff from them.

"Meanwhile everyone else probably works in advertising and so they

can keep getting paid to sit around Soho producing short films about the things in the shops that are clearly based on the assumption that I'm some kind of arsehole.

"And instead of taking a lot from a little, the government can take a little from a lot until such times as we all finally recognise that money is a ludicrous, man-made abstract that causes nothing but anguish and violence."

He added: "Now if you'll excuse me I was actually in the middle of recreating the climactic scene from A Few Good Men using half a banana and some Monster Munch."

Gypsies 'love stupid, pointless shit just like rest of us'

A NEW television series has been hailed for portraying gypsies as being just as shallow, materialistic and celebrity-obsessed as mainstream society

Travellers' rights campaigners and people who live in houses have praised Channel 4's My Big Fat Gypsy Wedding for showing that traveller culture, rather than being alien or threatening, is mostly about showing off and having more stuff than your neighbours.

Company director and former rabid gypsy-hater, Tom Logan, said: "I'd always loathed and feared travelling people as noisy, sorcerous vagabonds who'd steal your breath if they thought it could be 'weighed in' at the local scrapyard for its residual lead content.

"But I see now that they share my belief in conspicuous consumption and spending large amounts of money on flashy, pointless geegaws as a way of being impressive.

"Although I prefer to waste my cash on luxury consumer electronics and golf clubs rather than a robot wedding dress the size of a village."

Office worker and mother-of-two Nikki Hollis said: "I thought travellers lived in unsanitary wooden cars, did voodoo and let their kids fight each other with dead badgers.

"But I've now learned that little gypsy girls dress in sexually provocative clothing and get most of their aspirations from MTV, just like my own children."

Logan added: "I suppose I'll have to find someone else to victimise now and it will most likely be homos."

750,000 middle class homes could be forced to get Sky

Murdoch will use Fox News to fill his Guardian-reading subscribers with vomit-inducing guilt

SATELLITE broadcaster Sky's increasing monopoly on quality TV drama could force many middle-class homes into the murky terrain of dish ownership, it has been claimed.

Media analysts believe Rupert Murdoch's much-hyped new channel Sky Tasteful, whose schedule includes Mad Men, Boardwalk Empire and over a dozen gritty, complicated cop dramas, is compulsory for middle class people who need to be part of the zeitgeist.

Architect Julian Cook said: "The launch of Sky Tasteful has serious implications for me and my family.

"Whenever we have people over for dinner we love to theorise about the parlous state of British TV drama, and how the vestiges of the class system prohibits the BBC from ever doing anything with as much funky swearing and blackness as The Wire.

"But if Murdoch's new venture is going to potentially put my dinner guests several seasons ahead of me on Steve Buscemi's latest work there's a serious possibility that I may not be able to convince them I'm clever."

He added: "It's a nightmare that I'll have to subscribe, not only in term of class semantics but also because I'm passionately convinced Rupert Murdoch is the devil. Although if pressed I would be forced to admit I'm not entirely sure why.

"Possibly something to do with Israel."

A Sky spokesman said: "With an 'upscale' target demographic in mind, Sky Tasteful's receiver is not traditionally disc-shaped. It is in fact disguised as a wheel of expensive Brie-like gooey cheese labelled 'Le Coquillon'.

"Of course you'll still have to explain why you've got cheese on your roof, but that's your problem."

High street inquiry takes about four seconds

It has a big car park and sells loads of stuff

AN inquiry into why Britain's high streets are in decline has been launched and published in the time it took to read this sentence.

Shopping expert Mary Portas was this morning asked by the prime minister David Cameron to investigate why Britain's High Streets were becoming ghost towns and immediately replied 'supermarkets, parking, and rubbish shops'.

She then looked at the prime minister as if to say 'am I supposed to keep talking?'.

While she was saying 'supermarkets, parking and rubbish shops' Portas also composed a text message containing the same five words which she will send to the media and any member of the public who wants a permanent copy.

But the report has been condemned by MPs, sociologists, economists and the British Chamber of Commerce who all wanted to find clever, complicated ways of saying 'supermarkets, parking, and rubbish shops'.

Economist Julian Cook said: "I wanted to say it on Channel Four News. Boo."

And sociologist Dr Helen Archer stressed that 'supermarkets, parking, and rubbish shops' did not even begin to address the wide range of potential solutions.

But Portas immediately replied: "Fewer supermarkets, more parking and better shops."

The Portas Inquiry is the latest in a series of high profile initiatives from Downing Street, including Kirsty Allsop's quest to discover how cushions are made and a research project by Rick Stein to find out why no-one eats mashed, raw frog.

Osborne hands average family £45 to give to British Gas

GEORGE Osborne will today let the average family look at £45 of their own money as it travels from the Treasury to British Gas.

Mr Osborne wants to simplify the system by which people get less things in exchange for more money while boosting entrepreneurship by emphasising how happy you would be if you owned a multi-national energy company.

A Treasury source said: "It's easier if we just give the money directly to British Gas and send everyone a photo of their £45 in much the same way as one would receive a photo of a sponsored child or endangered animal.

"You'll then get a quarterly 'newsletter' from your £45 telling you how it's doing inside the wallet of a British Gas executive, what it was like being exchanged for an erotically-shaped cigar cutter or how it feels to be set on fire by a bored fat man."

A British Gas spokesman said: "We will wait for the exact figure before deciding how much to add to this year's price increases, but we do prefer to bill people directly and then watch them hand it over.

"It gets us very, very hard."

Mr Osborne is also expected to scrap a planned 1% rise in fuel duty after experts pointed out that 65% of nothing is nothing.

A Treasury source said: "We are perilously close to the tipping point where people will have turned their cars into houses and be using the rubbery bits to make sandwiches."

Other Budget highlights include:
● Three pence a pint on delicious foreign lagers that make you want to have a fight.
● A tax on private kangaroos.
● A £250m fund to help 10,000 first-time buyers experience the pointless stress of owning some shitty little house next to a retail park.
● A freeze in air passenger duty, clearing the way for Michael O'Leary to charge you for having a face.
● Meanwhile page 815 of the Treasury's 'Red Book' will contain the usual clause allowing rich people's lives to stay exactly the same.

coffee break

Your astrological day ahead with **Psychic Bob**

Libra
(23 SEP-23 OCT)
Venus and Neptune combine this week as you're arrested for going in to Sea World and exposing yourself to a puffer fish.

Scorpio
(24 OCT-21 NOV)
If absolute power corrupts absolutely then by rights you should be utterly squeaky-clean. However, a quick look at your internet browsing history would suggest otherwise. Donkey handcuffs?

Sagittarius
(22 NOV-21 DEC)
While you raise a valid point that Ewoks are no less ridiculous a concept than angels when defending your insistence on describing your religion as 'Jedi' it does not alter the fact that you are a bellend for doing so.

Capricorn
(22 DEC-19 JAN)
Well since my baby left me, I found a new place to dwell, it's down at the end of lonely street, called a brothel.

Aquarius
(20 JAN-19 FEB)
Men may indeed rise on the stepping-stones of their dead selves to higher things but you've found it an awful lot easier to use the backs of people you've inserted a dagger into.

Pisces
(20 FEB-20 MAR)
Standing in the terraces of your team's ground surrounded by thousands of people just like you is the last vestige of communal feeling allowed to the working classes in modern times and is a new tribalism replacing the regional battles that littered the history of early Britain. And you get to lob bricks at coppers.

Aries
(21 MAR-19 APR)
You cross an indefinable but unquestionable moral boundary this week when you start accepting requests from eBay purchasers that your second-hand clothes actually aren't washed before you post them.

Taurus
(20 APRIL - 20 MAY)
Your trusting nature is tested to its limit this week as you find your partner naked in a hotel room squatting over a glass coffee table and they tell you they're a furniture tester for IKEA.

Gemini
(21 MAY-20 JUN)
Take time at the end of each day to count your blessings – the time between switching the bedroom light off and the all-consuming darkness should be long enough.

Cancer
(21 JUN-22 JUL)
Well done – thanks to your new blog the written word has now become more devalued than the Zimbabwean dollar. Historians would have always wondered what your thoughts were on David Cameron, now they can see them in all their pinheaded glory.

Leo
(23 JUL-22 AUG)
Your grandmother was full of quaint little sayings that were peculiar to her but the one you've never heard anyone else come out with was "Back into the cellar or you'll lose another finger".

Virgo
(23 AUG-22 SEP)
Fame at last as you appear on Undercover Boss telling your colleagues exactly which piece of office furniture you'd insert into your chief executive if you ever bumped into him.

PSYCHOMETRIC TEST

Coffee break funtime with the Daily Mash psychometric personality test.

1. In general, you consider yourself to be:
a) Original and unconventional
b) The righteous Lord's soldier of redemption
c) Confident and self-assured
d) Spock's mother T'Pau
e) Agreeable and cooperative

2. Your ideal relationship is:
a) A bit permissive, you need your freedom
b) Worth fighting for - you love to win!
c) With the business end of a .22 Magnum
d) Secure and stable above all else
e) Being up to your knees in a piss-bath orgy

3. You really, really hate:
a) Having a problem no one can help you with
b) Not following rules
c) The people and cultures of the Asian sub-continent
d) Structured corporate environments
e) Not strangling donkeys

4. When things aren't going well in your life, you tend to be a little:
a) Arrogant and egotistical
b) Filled with the heat of a million fires
c) Cool and unemotional
d) Vain and superficial
e) Covered in faeces

5. Your friends would say that when you're at your BEST, you are:
a) Creative and open minded
b) Locked in a dungeon
c) Ethical and detail-oriented
d) Helping them bury a tramp
e) Thoughtful and considerate

6. Your friends would say that when you're at your WORST, you are:
a) Clingy and insecure
b) Demanding and self-centered
c) Reading this newspaper
d) Greedy and selfish
e) Conspiring with one of your 28 invisible friends

Okay, how did you score?

Question 1.	a)1	b)4	c)2	d)5	e)3
Question 2.	a)3	b)2	c)4	d)1	e)5
Question 3.	a)2	b)1	c)4	d)3	e)5
Question 4.	a)1	b)4	c)2	d)3	e)5
Question 5.	a)3	b)4	c)2	d)5	e)1
Question 6.	a)1	b)2	c)4	d)3	e)5

0-10: To be honest, you probably shouldn't be reading this newspaper.

10-20: Take one of the big red pills and we'll see you again in a month.

20-30: Someone will be along presently to show you to your room. Please remove your shoes and belt and place any sharp objects in the bucket.

SUDOKU
FILL in all the squares in the grid so that each row, column and each of the 3x3 squares contains all the digits from 1-9

Difficulty rating ★☆☆☆☆

Difficulty rating ★☆☆☆☆

Difficulty rating ★☆☆☆☆

Museum of Pointless Interactivity

Hey kids! Museums are boring right? All those old skeletons and pots and boring descriptions of things written by so-called 'experts' who reckon it's possible to 'know' things.

The **Museum of Pointless Interactivity** is different. For starters there's screens everywhere. Yes, screens. Like telly. You can touch the screens and they do things. Answer challenging questions like 'Is Slavery Good or Bad?' and see your answer appear on a colourful pie chart.

Or why not use our shiny computers, also with screens like telly, to 'Tell Your Story'. It doesn't matter whether your story is interesting or is just the word 'Fuk' – we want YOU to press some buttons.

There's lots of other things that are also a bit like telly, and a sort of plastic dial where you spin a spinner to make it point and a picture of some fruit. It's hard to explain really, you sort of have to see it.

Founded in 2007 by a quango of loud women wearing chunky beads and creepy Mandelson-esque men, the Museum of Pointless Interactivity is so now it's actually tomorrow.

Museum of Pointless Interactivity, Espedair St, London.
10am – 4pm, Admission Free.

Available to hire for pointless events.

PATRIOT QUIZ Coffee break funtime with the Daily Mash nationality test.

You are the England fan

Q1 You're about to enter a bar when a police officer advises you that it's full of opposition fans. He points out another, identical, bar 50 yards down the road full of England supporters clearly enjoying themselves. What should you do?

Q2 The weather in the country you've travelled to turns out to be a lot hotter than the travel agents had suggested. You've not really packed items for this kind of heat and don't have time to do any shopping before you head off to the stadium. What is the correct procedure in this instance?

Q3 After loudly proclaiming that this is "England's tournament" to the various nationalities at the bar of the hotel you're staying at, they get knocked out in the group stages after failing to score a single goal. What now?

A1 Kick him in the face and set fire to the premises before being bundled into the back of a riot van while chanting "There ain't no black in the Union Jack"

A2 Walk around in just your boxer shorts drinking lager, turning radioactively red and refusing all offers of sun cream or a shirt. After waking up two days later in hospital following a bout of heatstroke, tell the doctor to keep his dago hands to himself and hitchhike back to the airport wearing only your hospital gown.

A3 After running through the injuries suffered by England's fourth-choice striker and the obvious conspiracy by FIFA to put England in a "group of death" alongside Peru, Burkina Faso and Scotland, drink heavily until somebody mentions Bobby Moore and start crying.

Your problems solved with **Holly Harper**

Dear Holly,

I've never been much of a cook, but I wanted to impress my husband on our wedding anniversary by cooking him a delightful meal. Only problem is, I don't know which TV chef is the best to follow so I tried to create a kind of 'fusion' style like you see on Masterchef by combining the recipes of Gordon Ramsay, Nigella Lawson, Jamie Oliver and Hugh Fearnley-Whittingstall. Unfortunately, I ended up dressing in an inappropriate silk negligee and inviting all of the neighbours to join me in feeding my husband turkey twizzlers over the garden fence, whilst shouting at him to go fuck himself, which didn't seem to go down too well. Any ideas how I can improve my culinary skills?

Agnes
Melton Mowbray

Dear Agnes,

I'm afraid we don't get to do Home Economics at primary school, but my older sister gets to do it at the big school. I think that to be a successful cook you need to use a good dash of malt whisky in all your recipes because my sister is always helping herself from my daddy's special cupboard. I think whisky must be a special secret ingredient, because my sister told me she'd kick me in the fanny if I told anyone I'd seen her taking it.

That's not the only secret I know about my sister. I read in her diary that a boy from the sixth form gave her Chlamydia. I don't know what it is but I'm going to ask my mummy and daddy if I can have some for Christmas so I can be a big girl too.

Hope that helps!
Holly

PRIZE LETTER ★★★★☆

Dear Holly,

Things have been going really well with my latest squeeze, and I think we might have a future together. The only problem is that I lied slightly on our first date and told her I was going to be representing the UK at the high jump in the upcoming London Olympics. It seemed to impress her, as she let me pump her later the same evening, but it's slowly dawning on me that I need to come up with a plan to get on Team GB, and fast.

Do you have any ideas how I can avoid getting dumped and possibly win a medal in the process?

Martin
Swansea

Dear Martin,

Didn't you hear that story about Pinocchio? Apparently if you tell lies your nose will grow and grow and the only person who'll hang about with you is a weird insect in a top hat.

However, this doesn't always happen because I told Davina Sutcliffe that Ant and Dec came to my 8th birthday party and she totally believed me.

Frankly, it sounds like you've lied yourself into a bit of a corner, but perhaps you could try entering the paralympics for spastics instead and you might have a chance. Obviously you can't outrun a wheelchair, but I think you'd have a fighting chance of beating one over the high jump.

Hope that helps!
Holly

Dear Holly,

A formerly avid NOTW reader, I have been rather stumped about what to read on a Sunday. I love houmous and pitta bread, have several Le Creuset cooking dishes and love listening to my Coldplay albums. However, I also despise poor people, win prizes with my roses and never miss an episode of Top Gear. How on earth am I supposed to choose between the Observer and the Mail on Sunday?

Philippa,
Bicester

Dear Philippa,

The best newspaper is the one where you see naked ladies. I'm not sure which newspaper it is but once, when we were doing painting at school, we had to spread out the papers to stop the tables getting covered in paint and Oliver French found a picture of a pretty lady who was all puffy at the front. We all looked at her and decided she must have her bum on back to front. She looked quite happy though, so we gave her a green moustache and glasses but then Mrs Dodkins saw and took her away and told us that she's a naughty person. Oliver French said that she looked like the ladies in his dad's special book collection which he keeps in his bottom drawer, but he said those ladies all look like someone is hurting them so it's quite sad really.

Hope that helps!
Holly

Dear Holly,

The last few days I have been walking on air, having fallen in love for the first time in my life. Whilst I can't help but enjoy the heady feeling of amour, this is tinged with sadness as my lover is not a person but a golden retriever and I am painfully aware that people will find our love hard to accept, especially her owners, Margaret and Hugh from next door.

Is there any way Peaches and I can be together without someone calling the police?

Gerald,
Dulwich

Dear Gerald,

I love dogs too. My granny's dog, Bilko, has a special friend called Mickey who is a stuffed pig. Mickey and Bilko go everywhere together and Bilko loves to bite and cuddle Mickey in his bed. One day I saw Bilko rubbing his little red lipstick on Mickey's face and then he did a white wee wee all over Mickey and then licked it off. He does the same with my granny's slippers sometimes but she still wears them.

I took Mickey to school for show and tell and thought everyone would think Mickey was really cool, but after I told the story about Mickey and Bilko no-one would play with me and the teacher told me to go and wash my hands and then phoned my granny to take Mickey away. I don't get why Michelle Green's stupid telescope is so interesting and Mickey isn't.

Hope that helps!
Holly

SPOT THE LUXURIES

Examine the picture of this nest of scroungers and ring the six disgraceful luxuries that you paid for. (answers at bottom of page)

WELSH WORD SEARCH

L	Y	Y	Y	L	L	Y	Y	L	Y	Y	Y	L	L	Y	Y	L	L
Y	Y	Y	Y	L	Y	Y	Y	L	Y	Y	L	L	L	Y	Y	L	Y
Y	L	L	L	L	Y	L	L	L	Y	L	Y	L	L	Y	Y	Y	Y
Y	Y	L	Y	L	Y	Y	Y	Y	Y	L	Y	L	Y	L	Y	L	Y
L	L	Y	L	Y	L	Y	L	L	Y	L	Y	Y	L	Y	L	L	Y
L	Y		L	Y	L	Y	L	Y	Y	L	Y	L	Y	L	L	Y	L
Y	L	Y	L	L	Y	L	Y	Y	Y	L	Y	Y	Y	Y	L	Y	Y
L	L	L	L	Y	Y	L	L	L	L	L	Y	Y	L	L	Y	Y	
L	L	L	Y	L	L	Y	L	L	L	L	L	L	L	L	L	Y	L
Y	L	L	L	L	L	L	L	L	L	L	T	L	L	Y	L	L	
L	L	L	L	Y	Y	Y	L	L	L	L	L	L	L	L	L	L	
L	O	L	Y	Y	L	Y	Y	Y	Y	L	A	Y	L	Y	Y	Y	
Y	Y	Y	Y	Y	Y	Y	M	Y	L	Y	Y	L	L	Y	L	L	
L	Y	L	L	L	Y	L	L	L	Y	L	L	L	L	Y	J	L	L
Y	L	Y	Y	L	Y	Y	Y	Y	C	L	Y	L	Y	L	L	L	Y
L	L	Y	Y	O	Y	L	L	Y	Y	Y	Y	Y	Y	Y	Y	L	L
O	L	L	L	Y	Y	Y	L	L	L	Y	N	L	Y	Y	L	L	Y
L	Y	L	L	L	Y	Y	L	H	Y	L	Y	Y	L	Y	L	Y	L

4 letters
LLLL   LLLY   LYLY   YYLL   YYYL

5 letters
LYYLL   LLLYY   LYLYL   LLLLY   YYYYL   YYYLL   YLYYL

6 letters
YYYYYL   YYLLYY   YYYYLY   YLLLLL   YYLYLY   YYLYYL   YYYYYY

7 letters
LLLLLLL LLYLYLY LLYYLLL LLYLLLY LLLYYYY YYYYLYL YYLYLYY

8 letters
LLLLLLLL YYYYYYYY
Next week: Scottish word search (over 18s only)

SPOT THE LUXURIES ANSWERS
1: TV remote control. 2: Fancy pot plant. 3: Dining area. 4: Decorative fir cone. 5: Haircuts. 6: Children.

FACT CORNER

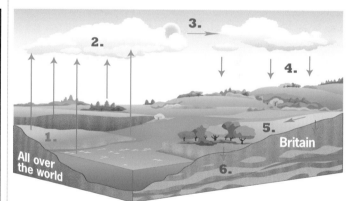

THE WATER CYCLE

1. All over the world, water lies around in the sun, dreaming of one day getting to spend the good life in Britain's waterways.

2. Through a process known to insiders as 'evaporation', the foreign water makes its way silently into the atmosphere and gathers in enormous gangs (or 'clouds'), setting Britain squarely in its sights.

3. Carried by winds from some of the world's most crime-torn regions, the water makes its way into our country, bypassing the woefully-inadequate Border Agency.

4. Once the water has managed to enter Britain, it's free to flow wherever it pleases, often settling on our picturesque mountains and hills.

5. By now, deep into the country's waterways, it can often end up in a reservoir and eventually people's taps. You or your children may have drank foreign water without even realising it.

6. Once excreted, the water now enjoys the luxury of some of the best sewage treatment in the world, without contributing a penny toward its upkeep. Meanwhile British water sits in ponds and lakes.

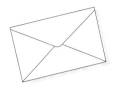

Need practical advice? Ask Mash!

Dear Ask Mash,
My cousin works for the dole office and he says that they just hand out claim forms to them as they climb out the back of lorries at Dover. Is this true? *Wayne, Carlisle*

Dear Wayne,
Not only that, they're given the keys to a brand new council house and a mobility car to drive there in. But just you try and get the council to come and have a look at your boiler and they'll tell you to go and tickle.

Dear Ask Mash,
Is it true the Queen can murder people because if she goes to court she can just find herself innocent? I'm sure I saw it in an episode of The Bill. *Gemma, Liverpool*

Dear Gemma,
All prisoners are there at Her Majesty's Pleasure, so technically she could go to jail but only if she felt like it. What many people don't realise is that immunity from the law decreases the further away from the Queen you get, so Prince Philip can get away with anything up to armed robbery but by the time you get to Princess Eugenie level it only really covers shouting 'wank' really loudly in a church.

Dear Ask Mash,
They breed like rabbits, don't they?
Tom, Sunderland

Dear Tom,
Not only that, but you can't turn your back on them for five minutes or they'll have your wisdom teeth out. Not that you can say things like that nowadays.

Letter of the week!

Missing - And Good Riddance

Dear Daily Mash,
Back in 1948, when I was a mere slip of a thing, my parents died of shame after finding out I'd gone to watch the film Easter Parade with a lad who had a touch of the tar brush.

I became forced by poverty to take a job at Lyon's Tea Rooms in Carlisle, where I met another girl there named Margaret who took me under her wing and let us sleep in her parents' loft when I got three farthings behind on the rent and the landlord kicked me and my three little sisters out.

We were great pals for the next ten years, maids of honour at each other's wedding and both our firstborns were named after each other. But we fell out in 1959, after she insisted she hadn't borrowed my salad tongs and I said she had.

Anyway, I'm a grandmother of eight now and the doctors recently told me that I've not got long left because my downstairs area has gone all off.

It's been over fifty years since I last saw Margaret or heard her infectious laugh, and I'd just like to say that I wouldn't open the front door to that bloody woman if she'd crawled there on her hands and knees begging forgiveness.
Thanks, Daily Mash
Elizabeth Turner, 79

Passed on: those we lost this week

Flat Eric
Fearless fashion promoter who devoted much of his life to blazing the trail for the 'one crease' denim clothing no longer popular today.

He was a keen driver, despite never owning a provisional license, to the chagrin of the police force who he sought constantly to evade.

Flat briefly pursued a musical career, collaborating with French artist Mr Ozio in the pop video 'Flat Beat'.

He died peacefully in his flat after a wardrobe fell on him.

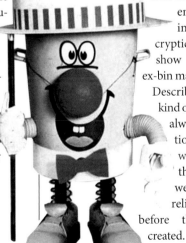

Dusty Bin
Upbeat receptacle and after dinner speaker who enjoyed popularity in the 80's on the cryptically acclaimed show '3-2-1' alongside ex-bin man Ted Rogers.

Described by all as the kind of performer who is always 'on' Bin's devotion to fundraising was so unmatched that he even took to wearing a comic relief 'car nose' years before the charity was created.

He was eventually phased out as television dumbed down and recycling became more popular.

He is survived by a chicken carcass and some used cat litter.

Arthur Fowler's Allotment Shed
Garden storage unit, who provided the backdrop for some of the most memorable moments in long running soap opera Eastenders.

Born 'Apex Larchlap Shed 8x6' the edifice changed its name to 'Arthur Fowler's Allotment Shed' after being assembled in 1984 by the show's production team.

Although critically acclaimed for its stoic performance during Arthur Fowler's bearded depression phase, the shed was also forced to serve briefly as a stash house, during the Daniella Westbrook era.

The shed never truly recovered from the producer's decision to let its allotment lie fallow for a year and finally lost a long, drawn out battle with some foxes.

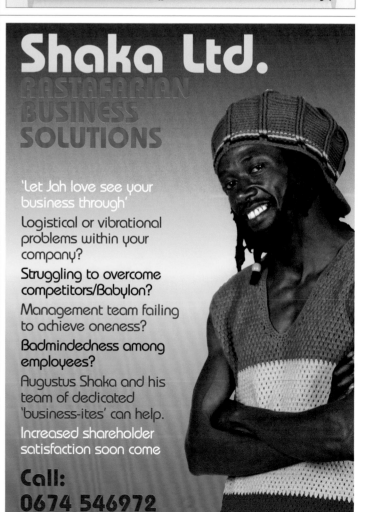

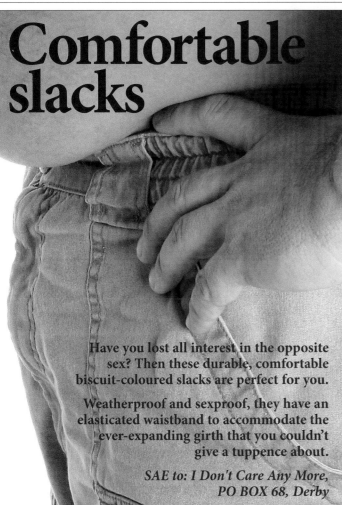

EMPTY CAKE COMPLIMENTS

For when 'it's very moist' simply isn't good enough. 500 equally meaningless and insincere ways to compliment someone else's cake.

Includes:
'It's a lovely sandy colour'
'The element of egg is perfectly concealed'
'So absorbent of my saliva'

Empty Cake Compliments by Claire Carter is available as book or E-book.
ISBN: 5436-3543-3634

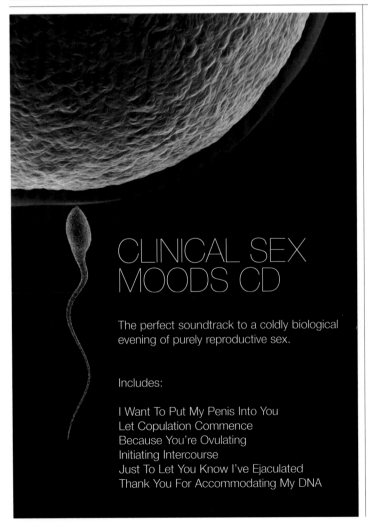

CLINICAL SEX MOODS CD

The perfect soundtrack to a coldly biological evening of purely reproductive sex.

Includes:

I Want To Put My Penis Into You
Let Copulation Commence
Because You're Ovulating
Initiating Intercourse
Just To Let You Know I've Ejaculated
Thank You For Accommodating My DNA

JUNKIE-LETS
Are you a smackhead looking for accommodation?

Or a private landlord looking for smackheads to come and live in your house?

Junkie-lets is the first 'junkies only' letting agency and the only one that gives tenants a free '£10 bag' when they move in.

JUNKIE-LETS, 45 Howe Court, Yeovil

Pensionertech Lightweight GOING TO THE

POST OFFICE

SHOES

Whether you're going to pick up your pension, pay something in or just to have a chat with the nice girl, you never know what going to the Post Office will throw at you...

Ergonomically designed to provide maximum support and performance for even the most gruelling journey to the Post Office, Pensionertech's purpose-built shoes are the cutting edge of elderly person footwear technology.

Impregnated with Neochron™ so that they're fine even in the rain, the chronospheric space-age lining will prevent your bunion from playing up while you're queueing, without restricting your ankles.

Journeys to the POST OFFICE will NEVER be the same again

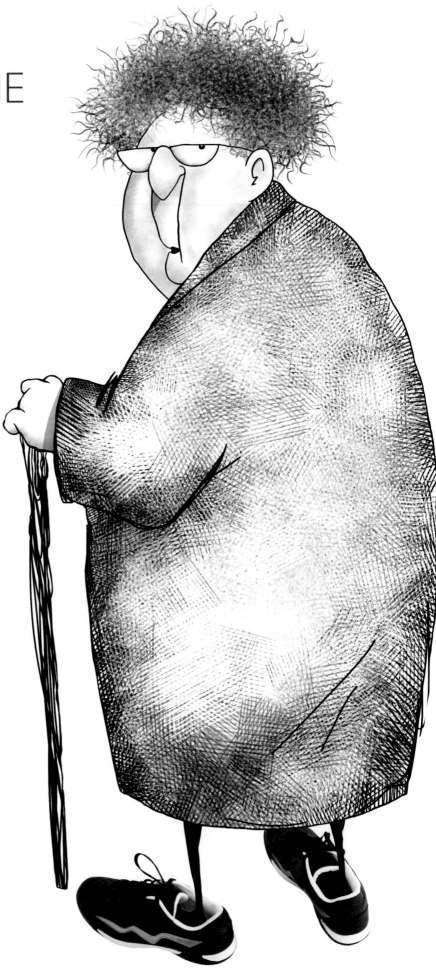

Pensionertech Lightweight Going to the Post Office Shoes from £68.99

Chancellor George Osborne at the dispatch box: "Fat, greedy piggy"

Osborne to stop bank bonuses with angry poem

CHANCELLOR George Osborne is to put an end to excessive bank bonuses with an angry poem about shame.

Rejecting claims the government had 'thrown in the towel' on City pay, Osborne said that when his poem was finished nothing would ever be the same again.

He told MPs: "This time next week we will be living in a new world, a world where everything is fair and everyone is nice. We will be living in the world of my poem.

"There comes a time in every statesman's career when he is faced with an issue so great that responding with new legislation is demeaning for everyone concerned. It is at times such as these when he sits at his writing desk, picks up his pen and lets loose the tiger that stands guard over his soul.

"Would you like to hear a little bit of it?"

The chancellor then reached into his jacket, pulled out a piece of paper, cleared his throat and said: "Fat, greedy piggy and his trough full of money. Oink oink, piggy, your nose is all runny." He then bowed his head before the hushed Commons chamber, folded the paper and put it back in his pocket.

As members on all sides got to their feet and began cheering, a triumphant Mr Osborne shouted above the noise: "All that is necessary for the triumph of evil is for good men to not write poetry!"

The Treasury later stressed the poem was the 'nuclear option' after a series of initiatives including writing to the UK's senior investment bankers and asking them how they would like their bonuses to be taxed.

A spokesman said: "He also met several of them in person and asked whether they could pay themselves slightly less money, but unfortunately they said 'no'.

"They were very nice about it and pushed him really hard against the wall so that his face was all scrunched up, before threatening to move their businesses to Bahrain and turn Britain into a slave labour camp/whorehouse for Chinese gangsters.

"Thank goodness we now have the poem."

People still unsure how banks work

THE £6.5m bonus paid to Barclays chief Bob Diamond was last night criticised by people with no real grasp of capitalism.

Angry online word-flingers roundly condemned the sum which coincidentally was the jackpot amount won in the weekend's lottery by somebody who did approximately 12 seconds' work buying their ticket.

Julian Cook, from Donnelly-McPartlin, said: "I will cheerfully give a weeks' wages to the first internet Paxman complaining about our bonus system that can even vaguely explain what it is we do for a living.

"Bob Diamond earned his bonus by maximising Barclay's equity differential market by a factor of six whilst ensuring their contingent capital base stayed under 2.3% Or have I just made all of that up? You haven't the faintest idea, have you?"

But taxi driver and part-time financial analyst Roy Hobbs said: "It's all about fat cats and bailouts, isn't it? We own Barclays along with all the other banks so where's my £6.5 million? That's the question I'm absolutely convinced I'm the first person to ever have asked."

But Cook stressed: "Arsing off about the capitalist system is rather like a fish complaining about the preponderance of water in its life.

"Unless, of course, you're somehow venting your dreary, uninformed fury on the internet via a computer made from twigs by a worker's collective.

"And complaining that bankers are obsessed with making money is like saying lions are obsessed with eating gazelles.

"Perhaps you'd prefer us to sit around weaving fair trade wicker baskets and then use the profits from that to lend you cheap money so you can buy all those things you simply have to have."

He added: "We could try communism but then Bob Diamond would earn millions from being in the politburo, only you'd know nothing about it because the newspaper has just the one story and it's about how fucking great your community tractor is.

"You could try complaining, just like you are now, but then someone who works for Bob Diamond would shoot you in the face."

Mobile phone companies step up mission to make world a better place

MOBILE phone operators have confirmed they will need more money to achieve their sole aim of bringing the whole world together.

Unlike many giant corporations which exist purely to fuck as much money out of you as possible, the 'big four' mobile companies re-dedicated themselves to making everything really groovy and making sure everyone appreciates how totally brilliant and special all their friends are.

A spokesman for the British Association of Making Great Memories said: "The world is one big, lovely playground, set to Devendra Banhardt songs about magical spiders.

"People keep saying to us, 'hey, you guys are way too chilled out, don't you even care about making money?'

"But we're too busy listening to Joanna Newsom in quirky places, while watching children blow bubbles and enjoying spontaneous group hugs with strangers, to worry about materialistic gain.

"Maybe that's irresponsible, but hey, you can't put a price on happiness.

"However.

Committed to delivering park-based good times

"We are hoping to give everyone in the world a lovely cupcake and a balloon, but unfortunately the price of cheerfully coloured cupcake icing has gone up.

"So we are going to increase prices substan-tially and you are going to pay. Unless you don't want to high five your friends when you meet up in the park for a game of frisbee that you wish would last forever?

"Just be nice."

Bosses of cold calling companies still refusing to kill themselves

THE call centre bosses whose minions regularly upset your nan are still ignoring demands to destroy themselves, according to new research.

The Institute for Studies found that despite a million passionate pleas, the instigators of 'cold calls' are stubbornly refusing to hop off a 10th-floor window ledge.

Professor Henry Brubaker said: "If you find that you are a bloated sweating tick in slip-ons and salmon-pink tie the decent thing would be to ter-minate your existence immediately so that your decomposing tick-flesh might at least nourish some worms.

"On the other hand... no, it seems there is no other hand. This is the only hand."

He added: "To clarify I don't mean the crushed drones whose sorry job it is to interrupt tired people's evenings in the vague hope that they might not have realised they want some guttering. They're just broke and desperate, and barely alive anyway."

Biologist Dr Emma Bradford said: "I was just about to isolate a gene which causes several common cancers when the phone rang. I thought, 'damn, I'd better get it – mum might've had a fall'.

"But it was someone asking if I wanted something made of UPVC to bolt on to my house, as if such a drastic course of action - as well as the means by which to make a reality - had not previously occurred to me.

"I said I wasn't interested, thanks. To which he responded 'can you tell me why you aren't interested?'

"To which I replied 'because it's a bit nicer than just telling you to go fuck yourself to death you scabrous ballbag.'"

She added: "I'm going to create a microbe that picks specifically on call centre owners, takes over their bodies and forces them to sit on something sharp and rusty while their organs putrefy to an excrement-like paste and spurt from their nostrils.

"I presume we're all okay with that?"

City News

Barclays bonuses don't fall by 33% 'because that's not how it works'

BONUSES at Barclays will rise despite a fall in profits because that is just how the whole thing actually works, the bank has explained.

Barclays half-year profits plunged by 33%, in part because the bank paid out £1bn in insurance mis-selling claims due to the company's executives being very bad at their jobs.

The rest of the profit slide was caused by a variety of other factors involving the company's executives being very bad at their jobs.

But the bank stressed that those executives would still receive generous bonus packages because that is how it 'works'.

A spokesman said: "We use a very complex formula to calculate bonuses, so if, for example, profits fall by 33% then bonuses would only go up by 72%.

"It should be obvious how those two numbers are related, but let me explain it anyway.

"What we do is we take the amount of money the bank has made, divide it by the amount our executives would like to earn, amortise that figure over 36 months, net of tax that will be avoided anyway, and then multiply it by the cubed root of not giving a fuck what you think."

The spokesman also stressed that many Barclays staff are talented and sought after individuals who either lend money at highly skilled rates of interest to people who are fairly likely to pay it back, or they skillfully buy and sell shares in profitable companies run by people who are not very bad at their jobs.

He added: "I hate to think what would happen if the people who don't work here didn't know what they were doing."

Britain urges RBS to take huge, potentially lucrative risks

Do it. Do it. Do it. Do it. Do it. Do it. Do it. Do it. Do it. Do it. Do it. Do it.

THE Royal Bank of Scotland has been urged to make a series of massive, insanely risky investments in a bid to boost its share price.

With everyone in Britain set to be handed a £1000 slice of the part-nationalised bank, people across the country are demanding a huge profit as quickly as possible.

Nick Clegg, the deputy prime minister and Vince Cable, the cleverest man in Europe, have devised the public shareholding scheme in what economists have described as the closest you can get to a cast-iron guarantee of almost unimaginable success.

Martin Bishop, from Peterborough, said: "They should invest everything in Argentina. Did you know that Argentina means 'the land of silver'? You literally cannot go wrong."

Helen Archer, from Newark, added: "Snakeskin will be the next big fashion tsunami. Everything is going to be made of snakeskin – trousers, handbags, aeroplanes. We need to corner the snakeskin market immediately."

And Stephen Malley, from Hatfield said: "I read an article on the internet that said there's a lot of money to be made from sub-prime American mortgages. It said I would get a 5,000% profit within 48 hours. I like the sound of that.

He added: "I can't wait to get the money. I'm going to buy a ride-on lawn mower and then parade around my garden like a fucking emperor."

Mr Clegg said: "I haven't worked out all the details yet, but it just feels right - don't you reckon?

"Personally I think they should invest it all in Japanese nuclear power plants."

Meanwhile former RBS chief executive Sir Fred Goodwin has said he will sell his £1000 shareholding and use the money to buy some magic beans, which he will then set fire to in the middle of a petrol station.

Bank reforms to make it look as if something is being done

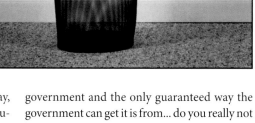

Chancellor George Osborne said it was one of the heaviest reports he had ever put in the bin

A PROPOSED shake-up of the UK banking system is to make it look as if someone is doing something about it.

The interim report from the Independent Commission on Banking sets out a series of recommendations based on their assumption that you and Vince Cable have no idea how any of this actually works.

Meanwhile the report has been given a cautious reception by the British Bankers Association in what experts have described as an insultingly transparent double bluff.

Nathan Muir, senior banking analyst at Madeley-Finnegan, said: "The central idea is that if a bank's investment arm fails then ordinary people's savings will be guaranteed and there will be no need for any more bail outs. But of course in 2008 deposits could have been guaranteed with-

out protecting the investment arms anyway, which suggests they have come up with a solution for a problem which did not exist.

"At this stage you should feel free to start getting very suspicious."

He added: "If an investment bank fails it starts a chain reaction of fucking things up quite tremendously, so the idea that everything will be fine because your little deposit is safe and snug in it's fur-lined box is what we call 'a lot of shit'.

"When that amount of money is lost it has to be replaced somehow, otherwise many, many other businesses will collapse. And the only guaranteed way of replacing it is to get it from the

government and the only guaranteed way the government can get it is from... do you really not know?

"That's right. And the reason you are the only guaranteed source of funding in the whole fucked-up system is because the government controls what we call 'the police'.

"So the idea that these reforms will save taxpayers' money in the event of a future banking crisis is like saying you will never get cancer because you always wear underpants."

Muir said: "You see, the thing we've learned from all of this is that unrestrained free markets are not possible without big government.

"How fucked-up is that?"

Around the world in a day and a half

See the major landmarks of the globe - and be back at work for Monday! Non-stop round-the-world tour from just £4,599 p/person.

It can be frustrating when your friends are talking about the wonders of the world they've seen and you can't join in because foreign countries equals foreign toilets. Plus you get burned to a crisp just on that weekend in Clacton so why would you want to go to a distant land that's even nearer the sun?

Becoming a cosmopolitan traveller used to involve complicated visa applications, a thirst for adventure and a willingness to talk to foreigners. But with World36© Tours, you can now tick off all the iconic and historic landmarks of the world from the comfort of your own plane seat.

Heading off from Heathrow, our team of British pilots will whisk you past the Eiffel Tower before you've had time to order your first gin and tonic. From there, it's just a short ride before you're zooming past Rome, the cradle of civilisation, at 35,000 feet.

For the next 32 hours you will be flown over some of the most stunning scenery the world has to offer. Whether it's looking down at the tops of the Pyramids of Giza or completing the whole of the Great Wall Of China in the time it takes to watch both of the Mr Bean films on the in-flight cinema.

After stopping off to refuel in one of the world's most historically-significant airports, you'll spend a restful night flying over America, before heading toward India to see the sun rising over a speck on the horizon that our cabin crew will identify as the Taj Mahal.

By the time you arrive back at Heathrow on Sunday evening, you will have been above 35 foreign locations that you can bring up in dinner party conversations for many years to come.

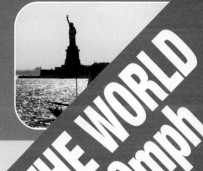

Benefits of the World36© Tour include:
- No having to learn basic phrases in foreign languages.
- No queuing for 20 minutes to have your photo taken in front of things.
- That day's newspaper.
- No beggars.
- A shorter holiday means an 82% reduced chance of having a screaming row with your spouse.

SEE THE WORLD AT 400mph

F1 is rubbish, admits Ecclestone

Nothing beats the romance of the Italian grand prix at Monza

BERNIE Ecclestone has confessed that Formula One is dreadful and he's sick of looking at it.

The world's shortest and yet longest midlife crisis has spent the last 30 years managing to convince people to gawp at a 200mph rollerskate that weighs less than your dinner and costs more than your house.

The deception has made him one of the world's richest men under four foot tall and has been described by financial experts as 'a sporting ponzi scheme with lots of big-breasted blonde women milling around for no apparent reason'.

He said: "Even if we make it rain spaceships onto the track every five minutes and tune the engines to sound like Kylie Minogue reaching a spectacular climax it's still going to be like staring at a stretch of the M25 but with an even higher concentration of tedious men with too much money sitting in pointlessly expensive cars.

"You can carry on watching in the hope of a really good pile-up but you may as well watch Eastenders in the hope that Arthur comes out of his allotment shed with Dirty Den's head on a stick."

Earlier this year Ecclestone drew up a series of ideas to make the sport more exciting, including the use of agent provocateurs to provoke a revolution in Bahrain and then attempting to stage a grand prix right in the middle of it.

But the plan was abandoned when a feasibility study showed motor racing was better at quelling unrest than a job-lot of tranquiliser darts.

Ecclestone now hopes to spice up this year's British grand prix by stopping it halfway through for a poetry reading by Sir Ian McKellen.

Boycott to open therapy centre

GEOFF Boycott is to open Yorkshire's largest psychotherapy clinic, with a pledge to cure a patient every eight seconds.

Treatments will include sock-pulling-up lessons and an automated face-slapping machine that will simultaneously shake patients by the shoulders while buying them a pint of bitter.

Boycott said: "You might be an absolute bloody disgrace of a man right now, but I promise I can stop you from crying like some old grannie and do it with my eyes shut.

"Before you know it, you'll be burying all those useless feelings under a steady diet of alcohol and bluster about car maintenance.

"I'm no psychiatrist, as every scrap of evidence clearly points to, but I do know that there's nowt that can't be cured by taking the dog for a walk while somebody tells you to pack it in because you're a damned embarrassment to the game."

The Geoffrey Boycott Depansification Clinic will not treat women because who really wants to listen to some bloody female going on about her emotional void and her dodgy waterworks?

But psychiatrist Dr Nikki Hollis said: "Boycott should try to understand that not everybody is from Yorkshire and as such may not have an unshakeable and wholly unjustified belief in their own brilliance.

"Most humans are prey to bouts of introspection and self-doubt rather than loudly telling anybody who'll listen that they come from the greatest piece of land on the planet and that therefore, by some inexplicable transitive property, they are also unquestionably superb.

"Depression is a complex and debilitating illness that sometimes requires therapy and medication rather than simply grinding out an unbeaten 152 against Worcestershire."

Boycott and his patented Pull-Your-self-Together Hat

Sharapova grunt awarded world heritage status

THE grunting of Maria Sharapova is to be protected under the United Nation's world heritage programme.

The move means Sharapova's passionate yelps will be excluded from a threatened Wimbledon grunting crackdown.

The UN acted after a deluge of panicked emails from lonely men who stressed the lithe, blonde Russian's intense barking constituted their entire sex life.

A UN spokesman said: "You can't compare a Sharapova grunt to that of some six foot-wide Bulgarian hermaphrodite. That's like comparing Machu Pichu to a shopping centre in Coventry."

Roy Hobbs, a single man from Hatfield, said: "I have a full-sized cardboard cut-out.

"Before a match I close the curtains, light some candles and pour some Pinot Grigio. Maria is impressed with my knowledge of films and then gives me a 'come hither' look. And that's when I switch on the telly.

"We then become one for up to 90 minutes of extremely heavy grunting."

He added: "I hate these early rounds because it tends to be emphatic, straight sets victories that last about half an hour. It makes me feel as if I can't satisfy her."

But a Wimbledon spokesman insisted: "While we have to respect the United Nations we also have to think about Cliff Richard.

"Do we really want him to go to his grave with the grunts of something that looks like a Serbian bodyguard ringing in his gentle ears?"

But he added: "I know what you mean about Sharapova, though. I reckon she's got something up there."

You may as well bulldoze the Alhambra

Cameron hails 'golden age' for lesbian squash

BRITAIN could soon have the best lesbian squash players in Europe, prime minister David Cameron said last night.

Announcing the first in a series of sexuality-themed squash development grants, Mr Cameron said squash played by ladies who are attracted to other ladies now stood on the cusp of a new 'golden age'.

He added: "For too long we have sat back as Spanish and Portuguese squash lesbians swept all before them. The fight-back starts now."

If the programme is successful Mr Cameron wants to invest heavily in specialised squash facilities for gimps, thumb fetishists, people who like to dress as their own grandmothers and Max Mosley.

Helen Archer, Britain's most successful squash lesbian, said: "This is long overdue. It's no fun when a massive Portuguese lesbian rubs your nose in it."

Meanwhile the prime minister rejected claims the grant was inappropriate at a time when no-one has money for non-lesbian squash equipment or run-of-the mill hand held dildos. He insisted the investment could be recouped by charging men to watch exhibition matches, particularly if there is a chance it might be leading up to something.

Mr Cameron said Britain could also emulate Holland where pay-per-view gimp squash is now the country's third biggest industry.

Olympic stadium to become 'world class' car boot sale venue

LONDON'S Olympic stadium will be transformed into the nation's finest car boot sale venue after 2012.

Determined to leave a lasting cultural legacy for the country, the stadium's governing body has accepted a bid from car boot sale organiser Roy Hobbs, who believes his events could attract buyers from as far afield as Luton.

Hobbs, who currently runs several car boot sales and a market stall where you can get mobile phones unlocked, said: "We're talking bouncy castles, a choice of up to four burger vans and of course loads of quality goods, none of them nicked.

"There's a woman from Rickmansworth who sells gingerbread men, she makes them herself, she'll probably be there if her shingles aren't playing up.

"And two smashing lads in a white Renault van with several hundred pairs of white size-7 Reebok Pump trainers that they got for their birthdays but unfortunately didn't fit."

Hobbs said the government has already been in touch about selling the stuff that used to be in the Millennium Dome and has since been kept in a massive taxpayer-funded cardboard box.

A spokesman for the Olympic Park Legacy committee said: "The Olympics are about pushing yourself to your limits and we hope that visitors will channel that spirit when they are haggling over a Poldark VHS box set or a book about how the pyramids were built by aliens, never giving up even when the seller insists he won't take less than 50p."

He added: "Athletics meetings will continue to be held on the site for the dozen or so people who are interested, so we're asking people not to park cars or vans on the track."

Police braced for velodrome stampede

LONDON police are urging people not to travel to the newly-opened Olympic Velodrome amid overcrowding fears.

Queues began forming early last autumn and by this morning an estimated 800,000 people had flocked to watch a sporting version of commuting inside a barn in the middle of a building site in the roughest part of London ... In the rain.

Pushbike enthusiast Wayne Hayes said: "I can't believe they only put 6,000 seats in the pleasuredome because who wouldn't want to watch Chris Hoy and ... er ... the other one that does the cereal advert.

"Still, at just seventeen and a half grand per seat, I'm sure it'll soon pay for itself with the many thousands of riding-a-bike events that we famously love in this country."

Crowd control officer Stephen Malley said: "So far we've managed to set up an emergency food and medical supply tent for the influx of visitors who just want to be near this magnificent cathedral to wheelies.

"Imagine the refugee camps during the Rwandan civil war but with them all wearing dayglo crash helmets and lycra."

Emperor of the Olympics, Lord Coe, has apologised for creating such a pandemonium of excitement and has promised the scenes will not be repeated when the Lee Valley White Water Centre opens in Spring with police warning thousands could drown in the hysteric rush to get a glimpse of a canoe.

Coe said: "This proves Britain is a nation that loves a wide spectrum of sporting events, that isn't just obsessed with the antics of 22 perverts kicking a ball, and that the Olympic stadia will not be windswept echoing monuments to hubris come August 13th 2012."

Volleyball SOLD OUT

Olympic flame to terrify Wales

OLYMPIC organisers have pleaded with the public to buy tickets for events not based on bikinis or hotpants.

The 2012 website crashed within minutes of being launched as Britain's men clamoured to apply for the various thinly-veiled excuses for jiggling.

Front-row seats for beach volleyball, rhythmic gymnastics and the warm-up area for the women's high jump have been most in demand.

Ruddy-faced Olympic enthusiast Wayne Hayes said: "I've applied for the most expensive seats as I'm going to need plenty of elbow room.

"I've always enjoyed myself vigorously when watching the games but to actually be there to witness the magnificent spectacle and be able to see every bead of sweat trickling down the....oh sweet Jesus Christ almighty."

Organisers are desperately trying to raise interest in the more heavily-clothed events with the introduction of qualifying swimsuit rounds for judo, three-day eventing and women's cricket.

Olympic fuhrer, Lord Coe, warned that without more flesh, tickets for events like fencing and archery will remain unsold unless local people are allowed to bring their own weapons and join in.

Coe added: "The Olympic ideal is to bring harmony between nations, but I don't see why we can't have loads of tight, hot arses bouncing up and down at the same time. And thighs."

Meanwhile, ticket helpline operative Nikki Hollis is fielding up to 200 calls a day from furtive, grunting customers asking whether they are allowed to pay extra to take home the competitor's towels.

She added: "Putting banknotes in an athlete's waistband will get you thrown out of the stadium."

WALES is to come face to face with fire on a stick.

As the Olympic torch parade route was revealed, experts said the sight of the naked flame in Wales would lead to either an evolutionary leap forward or total catastrophe.

Dr Julian Cook, an anthropologist at Reading University, said: "They may have seen forest fires – and of course there are the dragons of their imagination – but the sight of an upright human carrying a flaming torch will be like alien visitors from a distant galaxy.

"Most will stay in their caves, but the more curious and intelligent ones may try to examine it from a safe distance. They will certainly want to sniff it.

"And no doubt one of the younger males will try to have sexual intercourse with it, thereby learning a costly lesson.

"I would also imagine a group of small, tough females will be dispatched to Cardiff to form a protective ring around Charlotte Church, lest she become 'enwitched by the dragon stick'."

He added: "This is their date with destiny. It could open up a whole new world of cooked food and warm indoor spaces. Or, as I suspect, they will burn the place to the ground within about 20 minutes."

Meanwhile the rest of Britain is now dividing itself into those who are excited about seeing the Olympic flame and normal people.

Tom Logan, from Finsbury Park, said: "When we see the flame we think of Prometheus stealing fire from mighty Zeus and gifting it to man who then used it to forge new technologies and build a society that wants to watch a bunch of dreary show-offs poncing about a field."

Helen Archer, from Stevenage, added: "I do think it's great for the kids. It fills them with optimism and ambition and then, eventually, illegal steroids and steroid-masking substances that they will claim are just herbal tea."

Brian Sewell casts his eye over the twilight hours of the Premier League transfer window

'Lady Chatterley's Lover, portrayed by a Wookie'

AS one who has always struggled to maintain a full complement of staff that can attend to my various needs, be that preparing an elderflower and lemon curd 'toastie' at 4am or discussing who would win in a fight between Proust and Baudelaire (Proust had the superior reach, one feels), I have a certain kinship with the teams of the Premiership at this time of the year. And thus, I have perused the transfer dealings and picked out the Mozarts from the Salieris:

1. Fernando Torres
Liverpool to Chelsea
£50m

For the price of Rubens' Massacre Of The Innocents, the coltish Spaniard has escaped the Augean stables of Liverpool for the cultured sanctuary of Chelsea.

One can only imagine his sense of relief at fleeing the birthplace of Cilla Black, a creation I had the misfortune of meeting at a George Melly soiree in '73 and was a five-foot crystallisation of screeching common. Ghastly.

2. Andy Carroll
Newcastle to Liverpool
£35m

Costing the same as Van Gogh's Irises, however this transfer evokes a far greater sense of impending madness and suicide in the mind of the viewer. One feels that if DH Lawrence had intended Lady Chatterley's Mellors to have been portrayed by a wookie, young Andrew would have been the result.

My good friend the Earl of Carlisle is both a keen farmer and combatant in the sport of kings and some recent accounting difficulties forced him to part with his prized Arabian to purchase a more prosaic but much-needed Shire horse. Standing as Mr Carroll does at approximately 17 hands, I trust the analogy is not lost on Liverpool's followers.

3. Andy Reid
Sunderland to Blackpool
Undisclosed

The delightfully charming Ian Holloway, who puts one in mind of a character from Midsummer Night's Dream coaxed into a suit, has refused to discuss the price of this arrangement but it is believed to be almost as much as a camomile tea and a Chelsea bun at the National Portrait Gallery. Proof that Blackpool have more financial muscle than first imagined.

But I cannot approve of Blackpool as a resort ever since it became associated with that ghastly Middleton woman. Quite how she dares to insinuate herself into William's royal inner circle when I happen to know for a fact that her father can operate a stapler is beyond me

.

4. Merouane Zemmama
Hibernian to Middlesbrough
Approximately £200,000

I have absolutely no idea what any of those words mean.

Tevez to be bought for the nation

THE government has tabled an ambitious £50m bid to preserve Carlos Tevez for the entire nation.

Manchester City are considering an offer from the department of culture, media and sport that will see the creature placed in a cage atop a plinth in Trafalgar Square, Runnymede or Alton Towers.

Sports minister Hugh Robertson said: "It's important that we keep a native one alive and flourishing in the UK so future generations can tell their grandchildren they fed a lamb chop to an actual Tevez.

"He's such a magnificent specimen and I'm sure that anybody that takes an interest in the Welsh will want to see him up close.

"Oh, he's not Welsh? Are you absolutely sure about that? I really think you should check."

The government faces competition from Inter Milan but Robertson has asked City to consider the warnings of welfare groups who claim

He's like Vera Lynn

Italy has an appalling record in the treatment of Tevezes.

He added: "He'll be cooped up in a villa barely big enough to allow him to make a nest and defecate in."

"And rather than fresh, raw meat from one of Britain's excellent organic farms, they'll try and force feed the little chap some pasta, which he is simply not designed to digest."

Robertson said there were also plans for a national institute specialising in Tevezology and a scholarship programme that will teach depraved children how to chase down and devour an elk.

MATCH REPORT
South Sudan-4 Scotland-1

THE world's newest nation celebrated its birth last night with a 4-1 victory over Scotland.

The match was staged just hours after referendum results confirmed South Sudan's status as the latest country to be able to take apart the Scottish back four with a series of textbook passing moves.

The new nation's provisional government staged the event insisting a football match against Scotland would give the fledgling state a vital confidence boost.

The hastily formed South Sudanese Football Association then spent more than an hour finding out what football was before assembling a squad of seven players, five of whom had a full set of feet.

An SSFA spokesman said: "We were slightly disappointed in the scoreline and we need to do more to convert our chances. A 4-1 victory over Scotland should not give our next opponents a false sense of security."

Scotland coach Craig Levein said: "There are no minnows in world football anymore, particularly the ones that are only 15 minutes old and think a football may be some sort of landmine."

He added: "That said, there were some solid performances out there tonight and we did score a very good goal."

Football historians say the result will stand alongside some of the greatest Scottish defeats including Ruritania, Lilliput and the People's Republic of Marzipanistan.

Dalglish spends £8m at vending machine

LIVERPOOL manager Kenny Dalglish has defended his decision to spend £8m on a bag of crisps and a can of Irn Bru.

He fought off bids from rival managers who were willing to pay up to £1.30 for the snacks and sees the purchase as a sign of Liverpool's renewed ambition.

Dalglish said: "You've got to understand that there's always a premium for home-grown soft drinks like Irn Bru as they instinctively understand the British way of having lunch.

"Combined with the crisps – limited edition Marmite flavour so we really had to loosen the purse strings – it's going to go brilliantly with this corned beef roll that I picked up for £20m.

Assistant Steve Clarke has angrily asked why nobody was monitoring Dalglish while the former Chelsea man was away in Italy being shown around the remains of Aquilani.

Clarke said: "I thought we had learned from January when he was allowed out for an hour to see what was in the John Lewis sale and he came back with a sofa shaped like Andy Carroll that we've no room for?"

Dalglish confirms Andy Carroll still not certain to face sea of confused-feeling Geordies this Sunday

Carroll to face late homo-eroticism test

Carroll and former teammate Kevin Nolan share the warmth of each other's bodies

THE shire-striker left Newcastle for £35m in the January transfer window, in a deal that made thousands of potbellied men feel upset in a way they could neither adequately define nor express publicly.

Footballologist Wayne Hayes said: "Many Newcastle fans will have felt betrayed and jilted by his departure, followed by the awkward need to do some DIY immediately to stop their stomach churning in quite so disconcerting a fashion.

"Seeing him run out in a Liverpool shirt will be like watching the mother of their kids walk into their local pub wearing a coat some other bloke bought them.

"This is assuming their ex is six-foot-three and built like a tattooed wardrobe made out of meat,

but given they're from Newcastle I think that's a fair assumption."

Carroll will be put through some light man-crush training today by listening to a group of heterosexual men discuss how much they like the programmes of Professor Brian Cox.

If he comes through unscathed, Carroll will be more rigorously tested by sitting in a crowd of football fans watching slow-motion footage of Fernando Torres exchanging shirts at the end of a match to a soundtrack of Donna Summer's Love To Love You Baby.

Hayes said: "It's easy to put this down to working-class men mistaking affection for complicated sexual feelings when a player leaves, but if they felt this way when Peter Beardsley left, something's definitely wrong here."